Ruthann —

Hope you enjoy my "stories".

Warmly,
George

A Tale of Two Stories

Excursions into a Narrative Approach to Psychology

George S. Howard
University of Notre Dame

Academic Publications

Box 478

Notre Dame, Indiana 46556

II

© Copyright 1989 by George S. Howard

Published by Academic Publications
Box 478
Notre Dame, Indiana 46556

Printed in the United States of America

Library of Congress in Publication Data

Main entry under title:

A Tale of Two Stories

1. Narrative psychology

2. Philosophy of Psychology

3. Psychotherapy

I. Howard, George S., 1948-

ISBN 0-937647-02-0

Dedicated to Nancy:

You know I need your love — you got that hold over me
As long as I've got your love — you know that I'll never leave.
When I wanted you to share my life — I had no doubt in my mind
And it's been you, woman — right down the line.

I know how much I lean on you — only you can see
The changes that I've been through — have left their mark on me.
You've been as constant as the northern star — the brightest light
that shines
And it's been you, woman — right down the line.

I just want to say, this is my way of telling you
Everything I could never say before.
Yeh this is my way, of telling you that everyday
I'm loving you so much more.

Because you believed in me — through my darkest night
There's something better inside of me — you brought me into the
light.
Threw away all those crazy dreams — I put them all behind
And it was you, woman — right down the line.

If I should doubt myself — if I'm losing ground
I won't turn to someone else — they'd only let me down.
When I wanted you to share my life — I had no doubt in my mind
And it's been you, woman — right down the line.

Gerry Rafferty, *Right down the line*

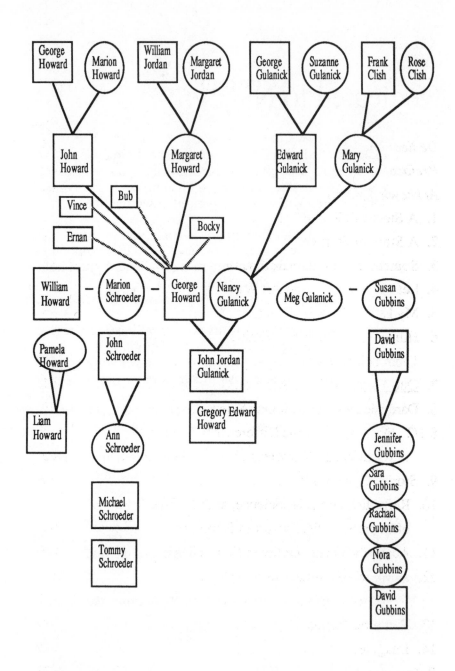

Family is very important!

Contents

                                                              Page

Dedication   III

Preface   VII

Acknowledgments   XI

1. A Story of George   1

2. A Story of Science   7

3. Sometimes Life Can Be Tough.   13

4. Let Newton Be! And All Was Light.   23

5. My Life as Seen by Others.   33

6. Humans Are Important Entities! Let's Study
   Them Scientifically!   43

7. <u>Quo Vadis</u>? (Where Are You Going?)   51

8. Dare We Develop a Human Science?   59

8 1/2. Do You Know the Difference between
   Wisdom and Knowledge?   75

9. Stories Gone Mad!   79

10. Reflections on Life, Science, and the Role
   of Therapy in the Pursuit of Happiness. . . .   91

11. Accuracy Versus Utility in Storytelling. . . .   119

12. A Model of Humans as Storytelling,
   Active Agents.   131

13. Pumping Karma   149

14. Imagine!   165

References   173

Index.   179

About the Author   183

Concerning the writing style of this book:

It is risky in a book of ideas to speak in one's own voice, but it reminds us that the sources of the truest truths are inevitably profoundly personal. Academics. . . very seldom offer themselves publicly and frankly as individuals, as persons.

— Saul Bellow

A man wanted to know about mind, not in nature, but in his private large computer. He asked it (no doubt in his best Fortran), "Do you compute that you will ever think like a human being?" The machine then set to work to analyze its own computational habits. Finally, the machine printed its answer on a piece of paper, as such machines do. The man ran to get the answer and found, neatly typed, the following words: THAT REMINDS ME OF A STORY.

— Gregory Bateson

Preface

This is the second book in a trilogy on psychology construed as a human science. The first book, <u>Dare We Develop a Human Science?</u>, dealt with the need to view people as self-determining, active agents in order to achieve a valid scientific understanding of human action. <u>A Tale of Two Stories</u> expands upon the theme of human behavior being primarily volitional in nature, and then suggests that the most important mechanism humans use to achieve volitional control is meaning. A life becomes meaningful when one sees himself or herself as an actor within the context of a story — be it a cultural tale, a religious narrative, a family saga, a political movement, and so forth. This book considers the role of storytelling in determining the course of one's life. The final book in the trilogy (as yet untitled) will probe the psychology of wisdom. Our current approach to psychology focuses upon *knowledge* of humans (roughly *how* people function). Wisdom (derived from one's purpose in life) deals with the question of *how one ought to lead* his or her life. Knowledge alone is insufficient to give purpose to one's life. Instead, wisdom should be sought from the humanities, the arts, and enduring cultural institutions such as the family, religion, and the schools. What psychology has to offer in our pursuit of wisdom will be elaborated in the final volume of this series.

In his volume on <u>Narrative Psychology</u>, Theodore Sarbin (1986) recently drew the following remarkable conclusion: "So, psychology is narrative." (p. 8). He, of course, was referring only to human psychology, and he explicitly exempted the part of psychology that deals with sensory physiology from his claim. So what part of psychology is narrative in nature according to Sarbin? Almost everything of interest! Is he serious in this remarkable claim? Indeed he is! Is such a radical claim at all defensible? I believe that it is an eminently reasonable and defensible position for one to take.

But rather than defending the appropriateness of Sarbin's claim that the narrative or storytelling approach represents a promising root metaphor (or organizing principle) for all of human action, I will simply accept the claim as if it were a fact. *What I propose to do is to weave some tales of storytelling.* In so doing, I hope to demonstrate the usefulness of narratives in illuminating such diverse phenomena as the life course of an individual person (me!) and the development of the notion of science in general — and a science of human action (psychology) in particular. Further, many applied psychological practices — such as psychotherapy — might best be understood as examples of storytelling, story-clarifying, and the effective rewriting of life stories.

The book is written in three parts. It consists of two stories and an analysis of these two stories. The first story is largely autobiographical (*A Story of George*: Chapters 1, 3, 5 & 7). The second story weaves a tale of the history of science (*A Story of Science*: Chapters 2, 4, 6 & 8). In addition to analyzing the two stories, Chapters 9 through 14 highlight some central features of (and issues related to) all forms of storytelling. Further, a vision of therapy as a part-artistic, part-scientific crafting of life-stories is developed. Finally, an analytic model of human action that is focused upon the storied nature of human conduct is offered. It is important to present such a model to highlight the fact that in switching to a narrative root metaphor to explain human action, findings from other perspectives (e.g., mechanistic, organismic, etc.) are not rendered irrelevant. Rather, they take on a quite different meaning from the contextualist perspective of narrative knowing.

If the issues sketched in this Preface have made you a bit suspicious that you are in for dull, boring prose about a potentially exciting topic like storytelling — take heart! The first eight chapters of this book are meant to be fun reading. We'll worry about the issues to be resolved (and the lessons to be learned) from the two stories in the last third of the book. So, for now, just lean back and enjoy a story of me and a story of science.

Here's a quick outline of the structure of the first eight chapters that you might find helpful:

A Story of George   A Story of Science

Chapter 1:
You meet me as a young child.
Life is simple and good. You are
introduced to a few important
influences and basic themes that
will run through my life-story.

Chapter 2:
The origins of science in ancient
Greece and Babylonia are traced.
We find that embryonic precursors
of several of the central
characteristics of modern science
were present from
the beginning.

Chapter 3:
I grow older and life grows
more complex. The simple,
naive views of a child no longer
are adequate to the complex
challenges of adult life.

Chapter 4:
The Baconian revolution in
science transforms simplistic
approaches to science into the
theoretically sophisticated,
empirically based achievement
of modern science.

Chapter 5:
Many other people have observed
my life closely. Here my parents
offer their thoughts about my life.
While one sees similarities
between their analyses and mine,
in several important respects the
stories differ. This exercise suggests
the importance of the
storyteller's perspective.

Chapter 6:
In psychology's first century, a
natural science analogue was
employed to understand human
action. But it is now clear that
this perspective alone will not be
sufficient, suggesting that a fresh
perspective — a human science —
is indicated.

Chapter 7:
I study my life at present, and attempt to peer into the future to ascertain not only where my life will go from here, but also to begin to answer the gnawing question of the meaning of my life.

Chapter 8:
Can there be a science of self-determining, storytelling, active agents? Of course there can be. But the first stirrings of this approach are only now being offered to the scientific community. We turn to the future to imagine the outlines of a mature version of a human scientific approach.

Acknowledgements

Thanks are extended to the American Psychological Association for permission to reprint parts of Howard, G. S. (1988). Life, science, and the role of therapy in the pursuit of happiness. Professional Psychology: Research and Practice, 19, 191-198 in Chapter 10.

Howard M. Sandler has generously allowed me to publish some of his thoughts in Chapter 13.

Portions of Chapter 12 have previously been published in Dare we develop a human science?, and are reproduced with the permission of Academic Publications.

Permission to reproduce the lyric from "Right Down the Line" by Gerry Rafferty was obtained from Hudson Bay Music.
©1978 - Rafferty Songs Ltd.
All rights for the U.S. and Canada
administered by Hudson Bay Music, Inc.
All Rights Reserved.

Permission to reprint the lyric from "The Rose" by Amanda McBroom was obtained from Warner Bros. Music, Inc.
1979 Warner-Tamerlane Publishing Corp.
All Rights Reserved.

Chapter 1

A Story of George

Anyone who hates little kids and dogs can't be all bad.

—W. C. Fields

It's a tough job to spin a good story — be it a story about some fictitious character, an institution, a nation, or one's own story. Regarding my story, no beginning sounds really appropriate — let alone as dazzling as some starts like "It was the best of times, it was the worst of times. . . ." So I guess I'll just have to start somewhere, and hope the story gets better as it goes. It doesn't seem that this start should have taken a week, and cost a pad's worth of false starts.

My memories of Bayonne are almost all good. I even savor the few bad memories, as they make the entire package more realistic. "That which does not kill me, makes me stronger!" Nietzsche was right — although horribly overstated for my tastes. But it would be a mistake to tell tales of meaningful lessons and blindingly acute insights — for that isn't the way it was. It was all rather ordinary — really. My memories are of good pals, exciting games of stickball and basketball, caring and hardworking parents, days of school that took forever, wonderful summers that raced past like the blink of an eye, and of Sunday afternoons that were so depressing that I was regularly reduced to tears.

As my British friends would say, I grew up in a working-class family. Everyone in my family worked — and our announcements of someone between the stages of high school and retirement who did not work were always greeted with mild surprise. By the way, school didn't count as work — it was a natural thing people of a certain age just did. I mean, you don't take credit for breathing, do you? Work was what you did after you took care of the expected activities. Besides, an idle mind (or body, or anything) was the devil's workshop. So we worked hard, played hard, and generally tried to better ourselves. But to say that we were an achieving family would not be exactly correct.

My older sister, Marion, and my younger brother, Billy, always were much better in school than I. In fact, it was widely agreed (OK, universally accepted!) that, while I was a nice guy and a hard worker, I was a bit of a dunce. While it goes without saying that I was saddened by this analysis of my intellect, I had to admit that all the evidence suggested that it was correct. But I was very lucky — being a dunce had minimal impact on my spirits. After all, almost everyone in the neighborhood liked me; I had lots of good pals; I could run like the wind; jump like a kangaroo; throw a baseball like Sandy Koufax; and, when we were choosing up sides for any game, I was always the first or second kid chosen. Hell, I was on a fast track to the National Basketball Association. You really didn't need to be a genius to be a star.

But I sure was a good boy — even in school. While I couldn't get too thrilled about getting terrible grades, I definitely wasn't going to get myself in trouble by making like I wasn't trying, or — worse yet — acting like a wiseacre. You see, I was born after the invention of the telephone. Those nuns wouldn't hesitate for an instant in calling up my mother and then I could kiss away play for the forseeable future (like a week).

If pressed to describe my grade school years, I would probably characterize them as being happy, safe (because I was in a very supportive environment), active, and simple. A word more needs to be said about why it was simple and uncomplicated. You see, we are talking about the mid and late nineteen fifties — the Eisenhower years! Did *anything* of importance happen during the Eisenhower years? When people reminisce about a simpler, less complicated time, I know *exactly* what they are talking about. The weightiest issues with which I wrestled were momentous problems like: having to do extra chores because I was late for supper; not knowing why everyone learned their multiplication tables faster than I; finding enough soda bottles to be able to replace the ball that had rolled down a sewer; and the like.

For me, growing up in Bayonne was like developing in a warm cocoon. We were all working class, Catholic, and of Western European ancestry (mostly second or third generation). In fact, my parents still live in the house where my mother was born. Families kind of grow together when they've been neighbors for sixty or seventy years. Besides, I had about a dozen close relatives (grandparents, aunts, uncles, and cousins) who lived within 150 yards of our home. As I look back on it now, I was never alone — I never had to face anything alone. Come what may, there were always relatives and friends close at hand to walk (or talk) me through any difficulty. It was many years, and many tears, before I realized exactly how influential that constant, early support was for me. I did work as a psychotherapist for four years during and immediately after graduate school. The most difficult clients for me to listen to (let alone to be of some help to) were the ones who had encountered severely traumatic experiences during childhood. I became paralyzed with an overwhelming guilt (because unlike them I was blessed with a wonderful childhood) that rendered me somewhat (OK, totally!) ineffective as a helper for them. Thus, the career choice to be an academic psychologist was easy — and I never seriously looked back. To give you an idea how idyllic my childhood now appears to me (in retrospect), consider my lone "brush with the law" as a youth.

> *My salad days, When I was green in judgment.*
> — William Shakespeare

I was driving home from a bowling outing with friends late one Saturday afternoon. I clearly had the right of way, but she pulled out of her parking space and her left front fender ripped the entire right side of my car. The only voice I could hear was my father's. A few months earlier (when I was awarded my learner's permit) he had stated *quite* emphatically,". . . and if you ever get into an accident *call the police immediately.*" As I phoned for police assistance, I was very shaken (from the accident) but enormously relieved that I knew "the right thing to do." The potential problems associated with my being a seventeen year-old who had gotten into an accident with the wife of a prominent physician in town, and whose learning permit happened to be in the pocket of another pair of slacks, were still a million miles from my awareness.

I began to suspect that I was in trouble by the look in Officer Jones' eyes when I discovered that I didn't have my learner's permit with me. I knew I was in trouble when the physician's wife suggested she and the policeman have a private chat. And I was overcome with nausea when Officer Jones announced that I *would* sign a statement saying the accident was my fault — and my insurance company would pay to fix our cars — or he would throw me in jail. All I was able to choke out was that the accident was not my fault, and that I wouldn't sign anything. Fortunately, the ride to the police station was sufficiently long to enable me to gather my senses — and form a plan. As soon as I was led in tow to the desk sergeant, I shouted for everyone in the squad room to hear, "I wanna see my Uncle Bub! NOW!"

Officer Jones had no way of knowing it, but he had stumbled into the jaws of our family's only *bona fide* success story. By dint of hard work and fidelity to duty for over thirty years, Bub Mahon had risen from being an ordinary cop, pounding a beat, to the chief of police. The desk sergeant tried to pacify me by suggesting that it wasn't "necessary to disturb the chief with this small . . ." "Get him now, or you're in trouble too," I cried. The sergeant, who knew an explosive situation when he saw one, wisely punted, "Chief, your nephew is here to see you." You see, Bub wasn't really my uncle (but yelling something like — "I wanna see my seventh cousin, twice removed!" — would probably lack force). And, in fact, I never called him anything but Uncle Bub. (That's not completely true — if I caught him talking to someone "important" [like a mayor, or a Monsignor], I'd breeze by and nonchalantly chirp, "Hi 'ya Bubbles!") And, in fact, he never called me anything but "Nephew George" (unless, of course, I had just called him "Bubbles"). I was proud to think of him as my uncle — and so I adopted him.

But getting back to the story, no sooner did Bub appear than Officer Jones and I began to blurt out parallel — but very different — versions of "the story." Eventually, I became so upset that I began to cry. I summarized with a sobbing, ". . . and, Uncle Bub, you know I'd never tell you a lie." And in that moment of silence one could almost hear the great court judge in the sky announce, "Advantage, young mister Howard." I silently thanked my lucky stars for all those times I had been compulsively honest with Bub. By the look in Bub's eyes — even if Officer Jones had been a cat (with nine lives) — he still would have been dead as a doornail. "Murphy! Get a squad car and take my nephew home. Jones! My office!"

About the fifteenth time I thanked Bub for "getting me out of trouble," and apologized for "causing him all that trouble," he said that it was probably for the best that it happened. People can be very cruel sometimes — and he was just happy that this time I was around friends when I needed help. As always, Bub was right — as I'd later find out. But more importantly, Officer Jones was young and would have to determine right from wrong as the representative of the law for many years to come. Bub was convinced that the experience was one Officer Jones would not soon forget — and that he would be a far better cop for it. I hope Bub was right.

If all this sounds like so much "truth, wisdom, and beauty," or piles and piles of "happy horseshit," then I'm sorry. But that's the way I remember it. I had more than my share of fights as a child. I also broke more than my share of bones while playing sports. But life seemed so good, so fair, so understandable, and so predictable — in the good sense. If you take chances, you can sometimes come up with the short end of the stick. But, in general, life wasn't cruel, or threatening, or unfair, or uninteresting. I charged into adolescence and young adulthood with enthusiasm, confidence, and more than a little naivete.

I've pretty much avoided what was an important part of my life at that time — my religion. Being a Catholic, for me, was a lot like being a male. I didn't know how I had become a Catholic. There was never any question about it — I would no more have thought, "Maybe I'll become a Protestant," than I would have imagined, "Maybe I'll become a female." And I certainly did nothing to earn the faith I had. (The catechism answer, "Faith is a gift from God," fit my experience perfectly.) But in Bayonne in the 1950s, being a Catholic was like being a human — everybody was one! I completely accepted the world view of Catholicism, and thus benefited from the warm, safe certainty that it offered. I knew right from wrong; I understood what was expected of me in life; and, through religion, I began to work out "my view of the world." I began to tell myself an increasingly more coherent story regarding why things were the way they were in my life, my community, and the world. As provincial, unrealistic, and idealistic as it was, it was at least a start, and that was important.

But with 20-20 hindsight, I can now see that the seeds of change were sown even then. It would just take a few years for those seeds to germinate. The religion I learned was liberally sprinkled with sin and damnation, stories of the fires of hell, and a deep suspicion of sinful human nature. I had more than my share of childhood nightmares of the devil and hell-fires. Finally, mysteries of faith were always my Achilles heel. Perhaps it was the first stirrings of the scientist in me, but even back then mysteries were puzzles, challenges, and mind-teasers to be dissected, analyzed, and solved. "Just accept it on faith," was the standard advice I received. And even if it was good advice, I was constitutionally incapable of heeding it. I simply had to think everything through — even though the thinking was painfully slow and frequently faulty.

I need to talk a bit about my parents before we leave the topic of religion. My father is a Protestant — although even to this day I don't know exactly to which denomination he belongs. He certainly never actively practiced. When he and my mother married, he was forced to sign an agreement that the children would be raised as Catholics. While there were times that he chafed under the terms of that agreement, to his credit he never seriously subverted it (to deliver an occasional joke is only human — and, in fact, highly desirable if the jokes are funny). But I know that I learned at least two important lessons from his example in the religion domain: 1) a deal's a deal (you agree on something and you don't renege on it); and 2) you don't need to be religious to be a good person and lead a good life.

You will hear more about my parents' version of my youth in Chapter 5 and more about my religious beliefs in Chapters 3 and 7. But, for now, you've probably enjoyed about as much of my grammar-school years as you can stand. So I'd like to shift gears a bit and tell you a different story — a story of science.

Chapter 2

A Story of Science

Science is an art — it isn't a science.
— Goethe

So much has changed, in the way people understand events that occur in nature in the last two to three thousand years! The shift in understanding is so profound that educated nonscientists, standing on the threshold of the twenty-first century, view the explanations of the ancients as ridiculously naive, and surely nothing that a serious adult could possibly believe as true.

"Oh! Listen to the roar of thunder in the distance."

"Yes, the gods must be quarreling with one another."

If the second comment were made by someone in the 1980s, it would be taken as a joke. But that same statement, two or three millennia earlier, expressed a reasonable explanation. Or consider another natural phenomenon:

"When I hold a rock and a feather and release them simultaneously, notice how quickly the rock falls to the earth, while the feather descends much more slowly."

"Yes, the rock moves quickly as it is jubilant at the prospect of approaching its proper place. But the feather is more ambivalent, and proceeds downward with caution."

Most educated denizens of our age understand that the noise associated with thunder has to do with the release of static electricity in the clouds — it is produced by lightning. Similarly, the speed of a falling body is a function of the body's density, the density of the medium through which it is falling (e.g., air), and its distance from the center of the earth. But even if someone didn't exactly know the role of density in an object's speed of descent, or that static electricity is implicated in the noise of thunder, that person still wouldn't have come close to falling for the "quarreling gods" or "the jubilant rocks and ambivalent feathers" explanations. Even though one might not know the correct answer, any intelligent adult today knows that the *form* of the answer is all wrong. That simply couldn't be the correct scientific explanation for the speed of falling bodies because science does not treat inanimate objects, like feathers and rocks, as if they had feelings, intentions, and emotions. Similarly, while an intelligent person might today still choose to see the "action of the hand of God in all things," that represents a religious belief and should not be confused with a scientific explanation. Science deals in the currency of natural physical causes and effects, not the whims and plans of gods.

So science has developed far better understandings of these natural phenomena. What is so startling about that? Well, nothing in particular, unless one considers how explanations have changed in other domains over the same period of time. In the domain of religion, the Old Testament was written at least four millennia ago — and yet millions of educated individuals study it regularly, and still believe that it holds timeless truths. Similarly, any philosopher who knows nothing of Plato's "Allegory of the Cave" or Artistotle's four types of causes would today be considered seriously deficient in his or her training. Finally, Aristotle's thoughts on good government and citizenship are still as fresh and contemporary as many current writings in political science and social studies. Thus, we see remarkable changes in the types of explanations that are now acceptable as legitimate scientific theories, but relatively little change in the types of accounts appropriate for religious accounts, philosophical analyses, and so forth.

An advocate of the special character of scientific rationality might claim that science represents a progressive enterprise (one that obtains theoretical understandings that get better over time — that get ever closer and closer to the Truth), while other disciplines do not possess this progressive character. This "story of science" will attempt to analyze the ways in which scientists theorize (or tell likely scientific stories) and the ways in which these scientific stories differ from the types of theoretical stories spun by other scholars (like theologians, philosophers, novelists, clinical psychologists, political theorists, etc.). So let's begin our task. How did early scientists spin their scientific stories, and how did this art of scientific storytelling change over time?

While it was difficult to find a way to start "A Story of George," I knew at once how I would start "A Story of Science." I had to put my cards on the table immediately. This chapter deals with the early roots of natural science. The material here will furnish the background for the most important epoch in the history of science — the Baconian revolution, which occurred during the seventeenth century. Of the four "science stories" I will tell, this first tale represents the domain where I have the least firsthand background. Thus, I had to rely heavily on the insight and analysis of others to guide me in my characterization of how the ancients understood their crude efforts, which, as we know, eventually led to the masterpiece of modern science. The work of my friend and colleague, Ernan McMullin, was most helpful. My story of science will be a simplified version of the story Ernan told in his Presidential Address to the Western Division of the American Philosophical Association in 1984. My story is to Ernan's address as the shadows on Plato's cave wall are to the light-of-day reality that we know and understand.

In telling the story of science, things become complex almost immediately. Historians are split as to whether the roots of science lay in ancient Greece or in Babylonia. But a world-class storyteller like Ernan cannot simply select one of these two stories and pretend that the other doesn't exist, for out of each tradition a different form of science emerged. Thus, I need to tell you both genesis tales. Had the sciences emanating from Greece and Babylonia been exact replicas of one another, the issue of dual ancestry would have been irrelevant to our story. But these two predecessors of modern science were quite different from one another. This fundamental difference and dual development represents an important stage in the evolution of our notion of scientific rationality. So we should look into it more carefully.

Imagine for a moment that you were a Babylonian scientist in the second century B.C., who was interested in the paths of the heavenly bodies. What would you think was your fundamental task as a scientist? Stated slightly differently, how would you know when you had made a breakthrough in astronomy? Readers with considerable background in philosophy of science will think, "Ah yes, George is asking us to consider the ultimate criteria for scientific rationality." Such folk can skip the next paragraph — the rest of you, on the other hand, might find the next paragraph enlightening.

You know, at no point in the history of science did the clouds part, and God announce,

"Listen up dummies! The ultimate goal of science
is improved human understanding — pure and
simple. Now it is important to identify some of
the ways that we will know when our
understanding of some phenomenon is getting

*better. By that I mean, we should have some criteria for knowing when our scientific theories are getting closer and closer to the 'Truth' — which is, after all, the best possible understanding — pure and simple. So, the working scientist should keep his or her eyes firmly fixed on the **epistemic criteria** — you know, things like the predictive accuracy, coherence, fertility, and so forth of a theory — in order to be able to judge the likely validity of his or her theory. The epistemic criteria are the best criteria (or guideposts) that anyone can find to guide one's pursuit of 'Truth' in science."*

It's a pity that the Deity never saw fit to make such a speech! But since God never told us exactly how we were to play the game of science, it fell to the men and women of science to evolve not only the ultimate purpose of science, but also the rules by which it is played. The analogy of science to a game can be illuminating, so let's probe it a bit further. What is the ultimate goal of the game Monopoly? To own all of the properties on the board in order to bankrupt your opponents. And along the way, how can you tell if the game is going well for you? One sign might be if you are accumulating money and/or properties more quickly than your opponents. What is the ultimate criterion in a game of basketball? To have scored more points than your opponent at the end of the game. Fine! And so we set up rules and procedures to be followed in each game to ensure that each team has a fair chance to achieve the ultimate criterion. But now the analogy of a game with science breaks down badly.

The early Greek scientists and Babylonian scientists seemed to be playing different games — or rather, playing the same game (namely, science) with *different ultimate criteria.* That would be like conducting a basketball game where one team wished to score more points, while the other team defined winning as having committed fewer fouls than their opponent by the end of the game. I can well imagine a game (albeit a very uninteresting game) where both sides would feel that they won the game because they were oriented toward different goals. But, as I said, this analogy is no longer helpful. Greek and Babylonian scientists developed different ultimate criteria for their sciences. Thus, very different *types* of science developed — but both were sciences nonetheless.

Ernan McMullen refers to the Babylonian-type of science as P-science, and the Greek version as D-science. P-science was aimed toward *prediction* and nothing more. The Babylonians believed that the gods were communicating with humans by heavenly omens (e.g., solar eclipses, the first appearances of planets, etc.). It was very useful for Babylonian astronomers to be able to predict in advance when these omenlike celestial events were to take place. By the year 50 B.C. Babylonian astronomy was extremely accurate at planetary prediction. But what these diviners/astronomers would *not* have asked was why the heavenly bodies moved as they did. From their perspective, that question had already been answered — the gods were sending messages. If Babylonian P-science is to be considered real science, it is due to its predictive power, its observational basis, and its computational techniques. The characteristic it lacked — which we now see as crucial to modern science — is the theoretical dimension. It made no attempt to explain why the heavenly bodies move as they do. So you, as an ancient Babylonian scientist, set your eyes on the predictive accuracy of your science. Prediction is the ultimate goal, the final criterion, the most important yardstick by which you measured the fruitfulness of your efforts. If some poor, lost Greek seaman objected that your highly predictive celestial calculations didn't furnish a clue as to *why* the planets move as they do, your response would be the Babylonian equivalent of "So what!" Imagine that you just sank the winning basket for Notre Dame over UCLA. You're overjoyed — of course — but the first statement a news reporter makes is "I don't see what you're so happy about — Notre Dame committed eight more fouls than UCLA." Your response — in English I presume — would appropriately be "So what!"

"So what," indeed. In ancient Greece, the game of science was being played quite differently. I could never improve upon Ernan's characterization of this difference between science as practiced in Greece and Babylonia.

> At a time when the Babylonians were still scrutinizing the skies for omens of what the gods would bring about on earth, their neighbors to the West were beginning to do almost exactly the opposite. They were formulating connected notions of *nature* and *cause* which would make the whole world intelligible in its *own* terms. No message from the gods would be needed; their intervention in the affairs of men would not be excluded but would effectively be minimized. Things have a *nature*, a regular mode of acting,

and a properly conducted inquiry can reveal the
principles of this nature. The goal of such an
inquiry is to *understand* the nature, to grasp why
the changes in question occur as they do.
(McMullin, 1984, p. 40)

Greek science sought to *demonstrate* (and thus the D-science name)
the true and immutable natures of the objects it studied.
Understanding was to be achieved in D-science when the search for
the causes of the action in question results in demonstrations that
reveal the object's true nature. Aristotle held that there were four
types of "causes," or four complementary ways of explaining
change. More will be said about these four causes, and how they
came to be understood in modern science, in Chapters 4 and 8.

McMullin shows the role of prediction in Greek science.
Prediction plays no particular role in a D-science.
Testing is not needed, since the premises are
intuitively seen to be true once their constituent
concepts are grasped. Of course, if the nature of a
being is understood, one will be able to "predict"
what the normal activities of that being will be.
But this is prediction only in a weak sense. There
is no suggestion that a *goal* of the science is to
enable us to discover some outcome we would not
otherwise have known.   The goal is
contemplative, a *theoria*, not in the sense of being
constructed in isolation from experience
(Aristotle's D-science is construed as resting
directly upon experience), but in the sense of its
being an intellectual grasp, an understanding, of
some part of nature. (McMullin, 1984, p. 41)

So there you have it! Two very different types of science:
one focused upon prediction as its ultimate criterion (Babylonian
P-science); and the other struggling toward theoretical
understanding (Greek D-science). While each approach evolved
and matured individually, many unsuccessful attempts (originally
by Aristotle himself) were made to integrate these separate
traditions into a unified science. But it wasn't until much later — in
the seventeenth century — that a compelling marriage of the two
traditions was engineered. The first part of Chapter 4 will trace the
wedding of these strains, in the Baconian revolution in science.
But first we will return to George's story, to see what you'd
probably already anticipated — that life isn't always a bowl of
cherries.

Chapter 3

Sometimes Life Can Be Tough

It's a rough universe out there!

— ALF

I really don't remember his name, so we might as well refer to him as Tony. I'll never be able to forget her name, so I guess we should just call her Marcia. I began falling in love with Marcia around the time we were graduating from grammar school, and by the end of my freshman year of high school I could think of little else but her. You wouldn't believe the elaborate daydreams I fantasized about Marcia and me. It was clear to me — and probably to everyone else also — that ours was a most special relationship. The darkest cloud on my horizon was the prospect of having to wait eight years (until we graduated from college) before we could get married. Now fourteen year-olds are not real strong on checking the fine print— even in relationships. So I can't certify that Marcia felt as strongly and deeply about me as I did about her. She certainly seemed to like me; she wanted to spend a lot of time with me; and all my friends said she really liked me a lot. It was ludicrous to even imagine that I could be so smitten by Marcia and she not feel exactly the same way about me. Wasn't it?

Well, to make a (potentially) long story real short, there was a high school dance and I was talking with my friends and somebody said, "Hey George, look at Marcia. She's dancing with some ape." Well, she was. It was this Tony guy. He was huge! Somebody said they thought he was a hood from Jersey City — but nobody knew for sure. He looked to be about three years older than me, so he was probably a senior—or more likely—a freshman who had been "left back" three times. Well, he and Marcia danced the whole night — and I did nothing about it. "Hey Howard, shouldn't you go over there and do something about that?" I knew the right answer — but I couldn't make myself do anything. I was rooted; paralyzed like a wooden statue. As I left the dance I felt depressed, betrayed, humiliated, brokenhearted, and a dozen other terrible emotions. I didn't want to see, be with, or talk to anyone — friend or foe. I was a beaten young man — beaten in love, in self-respect, and in spirit.

But guess who was waiting outside for me — Tony and three piranhas he'd brought with him. It was clear Tony was dying to fight — and I never wanted to avoid a fight more in my life. You see, there was nothing to fight for. Marcia had had a grand old time for herself. If she had given the slightest signal that she wanted to get away from that ape, I would have gone over and helped her out. But it was clear that things were proceeding exactly as she wanted. So there I was — feeling more hollow and vulnerable than I ever had in my life — and I was supposed to fight this cretin. He hurled every derisive, provocative insult that an IQ of 64 can generate. But frankly, anger and fighting were millions of miles away from me. If he wanted to hit the human equivalent of a sack of wheat — fine, go ahead.

Well, Tony never got a chance to have his fight. Jimmy and Micky Hart were neighbors. I played ball with their younger brother Gerry — and when they went on vacation I delivered their *Bayonne Times* route, and if we visited my grandmother on weekends, Gerry would deliver my *Newark Sunday News* route. If Tony and his boys were piranhas, the Harts were sharks. Jimmy mentioned something about them slithering back to Jersey City — and they did. You see, even piranhas know they have to watch their dorsal fins when swimming in shark-infested waters. I probably mumbled something like "Thanks, guys" to the Harts, and I must have gotten home somehow, but I honestly don't remember another thing about that night.

Even though I never saw Tony again, I somehow felt less safe knowing he — and others like him — were around. It wasn't until after it happened that I realized how vulnerable I was because I had been "in love" with Marcia. While love is heaven when you're in it, I was devastated by the realization of its potential drawbacks. I was frightened by the lability of my own emotions. I went from reveling in fantasies of undying love one moment to never wanting to see that hussy again in my life the next. And finally, I hated having the entire misadventure occur in public. While the epsiode probably lasted less than a week in everyone else's mind, I stewed over it for about another three years. Strike that — I'm writing about it twenty-five years later — this stew is seriously overdone.

Family and religion were two important parts of my life through my college years. As I was finishing high school, I wondered if I might not have a religious vocation. I saw the movie "MacArthur" recently and, apparently, MacArthur was fixated on "duty, honor, and country." So he went to West Point. Makes sense. For me it was "duty, God, and education." So I entered the novitiate of an order of teaching religious — the Marist brothers. My parents didn't want me to enter the novitiate —they wanted me to complete college first, and then try religious life. But as with all my life decisions, they told me their opinions and then urged me to decide what to do for myself. I entered. They supported my choice as enthusiastically as their disappointment would allow. They did their best. You can't ask for more than that.

Religious life was a very interesting experience — and I stayed in the Order for six years. Overall, it was a wonderful experience for me — and a good time of my life. But you'll probably miss that reality, because I intend to focus upon the reasons I chose to leave. I guess I ought to tell you the bottom line up front — I had to leave the Marist brothers because I lost my faith. My belief in God had always been a natural, strong, and sustaining part of my life. As a senior in college, one day at Mass it hit me that I could no longer imagine God any more. I'll try to suggest some reasons why this shift in perspective might have occurred, but the truth is that I really don't know. Faith left as mysteriously as it had come.

Why? Well, I can list some things that I know didn't help my faith at all. I took a psychology course in which we read Sigmund Freud's *The Future of an Illusion* and a philosophy course in which we read William James' *The Varieties of Religious Experience*. I found both books (and subsequent discussions about them) very unsettling. I knew it was coming with *The Future of an Illusion* but I was a newly declared psychology major, and I couldn't start off by refusing to consider certain parts of psychology just because they might threaten my faith. Besides, it never really seriously occurred to me that I might possibly lose it. Ah — the invincibility of youth. The impact of the *Varieties* experience came as a bit of a surprise. I took the course because the teacher (nicknamed "The Dragon") said James' ideas would be "an uplifting experience" for me. While James' ideas might indeed be uplifting, the Dragon was a bummer. Too bad I couldn't see the uplifting forest because of one downer tree. I also realized that nicknames are not randomly assigned to people — all too often they are hard-earned and richly deserved.

Speaking of people making it tougher to maintain one's belief in God, while in the novitiate our pastoral needs were met by the Redemptorist monastery just up the road. Thus we were treated to a strange parade of representatives of God. We either had old priests who'd been put out to pasture or rookie priests who were in the process of making (and, hopefully, learning from) their rookie mistakes. I can't tell you the number of times I counted the fingers on my hand over-and-over again, just to keep my mind off the content of the homily. One time I failed and wondered (aloud) whether the sermon was the proper place for "thinly veiled political biases." Interrupting a homily is rarely a good idea — for a monk-in-training it is always a not-very-good idea. I had to be punished — but it was really no problem. I could tell my superiors' hearts weren't in it. You see, those were the troubling days of the late sixties, when almost everyone doubted whether he or she would ever again be able to tell right from wrong. I think my Marist friends rightly saw my actions as manifestations of a wrenching soul-searching process that included far more than issues of religion.

Vietnam was a black cloud that hung over my college years. I was a senior when the Kent State tragedy occurred. But through it all I had a curious feeling of guilt. You see, in the draft lottery my birthday, June 8th, came up 366th. I knew I would never have to go — but I felt very guilty that many of my friends were so much less lucky than I. Upon hearing that I was number 366, I was so relieved that I blurted out "Three hundred and sixty-six! That's the special women-and-children-first category." It seemed like a harmless joke, but no sooner had I said it, than I realized that my single and double digit lottery number friends would fail to appreciate the humor — because for them the issue had a life-or-death seriousness. That's the thing about whether or not a joke is funny — it often comes down to whose ox is being gored.

But there were other tensions also. Those were the years immediately after Vatican Council II, and all religious orders were in chaos — we Marists were no exception. I was trying to develop an identity as a Marist brother at a time when the identity of the Marist brothers was undergoing wrenching changes. I think there are only two monks left in my class — which started with a group of forty.

Finally, death touched my life closely for the first time. My mother's brother — Uncle Bocky — died in an automobile accident. He was driving along a two-lane highway and an oncoming drunk driver crossed into his lane. Bocky got completely off the road on the right shoulder to avoid him, but the crash was head on. If Bocky had simply stayed in his lane — the car might have whizzed past on his right. But hindsight is always perfect. Bocky never married, and he had enormous physical problems (shrapnel in the eyes in World War II, four-fifths of his stomach was removed due to ulcers), and so his attitude was often bad — to others. But he never showed that side to me — we were always best buddies. Bocky played favorites — no doubt about it — and I was perhaps his most favorite.

We probably became a team when I was having enormous difficulties in grammar school. He took summers off and tutored me. Bocky taught high school, so he could get summers off. But wait a minute — that makes him sound too good. He helped me study in the early morning. By 10 A.M. we were on the Stamford, N.Y., golf course. Bocky spent more time on a golf course — with less success — than any human being who ever lived. Simply put — he was terrible. But for two kids raised in Bayonne (Bocky and me) a golf course was as close to heaven as we'd ever get. And since no one gets rich being a high school teacher, golf was an expensive habit for Bocky. Membership, green fees, a drink in the 19th, and *six to eight* lost balls per round — we're talking big bucks. Oh, did I mention that I never golfed with Bocky? I was his "caddy." But I rarely carried his clubs. You see, I was a professional ball-retriever. I was a ten-ball swing in Bocky's game. Instead of losing six to eight balls per round, we'd come home two to four balls to the good. Ponds and streams were as close to a swim as I was going to get — and woods and thickets weren't hazards, they were challenges. The Stanford club pro never referred to me as anything but "the Bayonne Bloodhound." And he took a dim view of anyone who slowly waded through water hazards — rather than walking around them. One time the pro gave me a hard time and pointed out that most caddies are employed to carry clubs — not to contract poison ivy. Well, Bocky heard him, and he just wasted him. I'd love to tell you exactly what he said, but that would completely blow any chances of getting a *nihil obstat* for this book. You see, Bocky's bite could be worse than almost anyone else's bark.

But, getting back to my story, in my senior year of college, things were very tough. I was graduating a year early, so I had to take 24 credit hours (15 is normal) that Spring semester and it was killing me. A Friday morning in late April, I was just trying to drag my ass to classes one more day to make the weekend, when a dorm-mate said, "George, a guy downstairs says he's Arnie Palmer and he definitely is not. He wants you to come downstairs — and bring your golf clubs." Sure enough! "Bocky, what are you doing here? Why aren't you working?" "Teacher's convention! Where are your sticks? Come on it's almost 10 A.M. and I want to get twenty-seven holes in today." After three and a half years of religious life — finally — a command I was thrilled to obey. Well, to make a very enjoyable story very short, Bocky left after four days — and over one hundred holes later — to "see if that convention is still in session." About a week later — at Bocky's funeral — I was telling my mother how incredibly lucky I was that Bocky had had that convention. There was no convention (she confessed); she had spoken with me a week earlier and she was very concerned that I was pushing myself too hard. So she called her brother for reassurance — as she always did. And, as always, she got it: "Don't worry, Sis, he'll be just fine." One strong belief in my family has always been — if you want something to happen, make it happen! But I digress.

A few months later, I realized for the first time that I no longer believed in God. Beliefs that were so natural and self-evident all my life were no longer possible. As mysteriously as religion had come — it went. I continued the life of a religious for almost two more years. Of course, I spent thousands of hours praying and discussing my inability to believe with friends and religious superiors, but nothing changed. Religious life makes no sense at all without a strong belief in God — so I had to leave. I was truly sad to leave the Marists, and they hated losing me. You probably have a hunch as to why I lost my faith — and if you're right, then you're a better analyst than I, because to this day I still don't know what happened. I left the East Coast for the first time in my life, and began graduate studies in psychology at Southern Illinois University. For the first time in my life, I was truly "on my own" in many, many ways.

The theme of this chapter deals with some "bad times" in my life. You've probably guessed by now that the good times weren't as uniformly good as I depicted in Chapter 1, and my young adult years weren't as consistently troublesome as this chapter implies. But a theme's a theme — so I'm going to speed by my graduate school years in Carbondale, my predoctoral internship at Duke University, and my postdoctoral year at Wichita State University. Why? Because they were wonderful times! I worked hard, learned a lot, began to form my professional identity, made many wonderful friendships, and best of all, I met (and married) my wife, Nancy.

But then I took my first tenure-line job at the University of Houston — "It was the best of times, it was the worst of times. . ." The people who hired me — primarily Ken Laughery and Rick Kasschau — genuinely wanted to do something to improve the poor quality of undergraduate instruction at UH. In addition to being an outstanding teacher (if one can believe teaching excellence awards), I had an extensive background in teaching evaluation and improvement — so I was a natural for their job. And it seemed good for me also, as I was much more interested in teaching than research. While I was a member of the clinical psychology faculty, I was to devote most of my efforts toward improving teaching in their enormous undergraduate program. And the usual promises were made that "if I was successful in these endeavors, I would receive tenure for them." These weren't lies — *per se*. If Laughery and Kasschau had been in power when I came up for tenure, I would have received it in an instant. But other friends on the faculty quickly pointed out that: 1) Laughery would not be department chair when I came up for tenure; 2) the faculty as a whole were not interested in quality undergraduate education; and 3) the upper administration was hell-bent on going from "Cougar High" to "Harvard on the Bayou." Research, not teaching, was what would get one tenured. Their points were well taken, so I fired up my research program. Since no one had purposely tried to mislead or deceive me, the voiding of my initial job agreement did not bother me terribly. Besides, I had good research instincts, skills, and some interest in doing research — so off I went in my investigations. By the way, I kept up my teaching improvement efforts also — I simply worked seventy hours every week. Since Nancy also worked seventy-hour weeks, it wasn't a hardship on our relationship. The nonwork time we had together was good — so we were both free to be happy workaholics.

Well, to make a long, sad story short, my research program flourished beyond anyone's expectation. By tenure time, my research credentials were very good — every faculty committee, departmental, college, and university, voted positively on my candidacy. But by that time the administration of the department had fallen into the hands of people with whom I disagreed on issues of intellectual, professional, and ethical values. They had to get rid of me because I would always be opposed to their vision of psychology, the university, and perhaps life itself. Besides, I occupied a position that could be filled by a loyal true-believer. It was just politics — really. But as I said earlier, how it feels is often a question of whose ox is being gored. In this case it was my ox. Besides, in a divorce if one is told, "I'm sorry, we just grew apart," one almost has to take it personally. That's just part of the way people are constructed. So things got ugly. One of the reasons it got bad is because the departmental chair had to be supported by the dean and the dean by the provost. But it would be very difficult for the upper levels of administrators to reject a set of credentials that said excellent teacher, researcher, and university citizen, and then deny tenure because they just don't like where he stands on theoretical and value issues. By the way, I would have loved to have had the opportunity to discuss those value differences at length with members of the board of trustees, state legislators, and any other interested parties. As if you haven't noticed, I still feel strongly about those issues. So the administrators had to construct a plausible scenario of "how it was that George didn't quite measure up to their high standards." It was doubly tough taking that abuse from a departmental chairman whose total scholarly output in quality journals for his entire career did not equal my output for any single year of the past decade. But I had to live with this nonsense for several months.

Nancy was wonderful during this time. She was the only family I had in Houston. Bub, Bocky, and Vince Harren (whom you'll meet later) were my protectors from earlier episodes — but by this time they were all dead. And so no protector arose — I was on my own, and I felt as lonely and vulnerable as I had in my entire life. I didn't want to bring my parents into it (I didn't want to upset them — and besides, what could they do?), I had no God to whom I could turn (that would be hypocritical), and aside from Nancy I had no life outside of work. As work goes (for a workaholic) so goes your life. And life was going none too well at this point in time.

As Nancy always says, "When the going gets tough — the tough go shopping!" So I went shopping for a job. I was plenty marketable, but the real rub was Nancy. She had a wonderful private practice in Houston — and she didn't want to leave it. You don't just pack up a practice and take it across the country. And that is what hurt me the most — if I don't get tenure, Nancy suffers. But perhaps her greatest strength is her flexibility. She said that she would like to get closer to home. So if I were able to get a job within a hundred-mile radius of Chicago, she might be willing to leave her practice in Houston for it. I grabbed the *APA Monitor* and the *Rand-McNally Road Atlas*. There was only one job possible: Department of Psychology; University of Notre Dame; Notre Dame, Indiana — ninety-five miles from that Windy City.

"Hello! George Howard, please."

"Speaking."

"George, I'm the head of the search committee for the counseling position at Notre Dame. We just received your credentials, and they come real close to what we're looking for. What would it take to bring you to Notre Dame?"

"Well, an invitation would be nice."

The decision wasn't hard. Our interview went well, they offered Nancy a job also, and by the time I returned to Houston it was clear the department was in serious trouble. (Within a two-year period Scott Maxwell and I left for Notre Dame; Jim Terborg went to the University of Oregon; Ken Laughery took an endowed chair at Rice University; Charlie and Lynette Cofer went to the University of North Carolina; Rich Arvey went to the University of Minnesota; and Mary Carol Day took a job as a research scientist at AT&T. Those are not, in my opinion, parallel moves.)

"Hello Mom. It's George."

"Hi! Where have you guys been? We've been calling but getting no answer."

"We've been traveling. Mom, I didn't want to bring this up until we had something definite. We're leaving Houston. Nancy and I have just accepted jobs at Notre Dame."

"Oh my God! Has Catholic education deteriorated that badly?"

"Mom!???!!?"

"Oh honey, I'm only making a joke. Of course, I'm delighted for both of you. Boy, your sense of humor has just gone to hell-in-a-handbasket lately."

"Well, things here have been rough recently. I haven't had a whole lot to laugh about lately."

"You do now!"

Chapter 4

Let Newton Be!
And All Was Light.

The knowledge of the world is only to be
acquired in the world, and not in a closet.

— The Earl of Chesterfield

Evolution can sometimes be cruel. Genetic mutations, that might under different circumstances bestow selective advantage upon their host organism, are sometimes unlucky enough to fall upon inhospitable ecological niches. The poor devils die off, and often are lost from the historical record — they simply do not become another step toward the species that eventually evolves. This is also the way it is in the evolution of ideas in science. For many centuries, bright, dedicated scientists (like the great Alexandrian astronomer Ptolemy) struggled to integrate Babylonian P-science with Greek D-science. Alas, either their insights were inadequate, or the intellectual climate was unready for their good insights, or both. But for many thousands of years, the integration of P-science and D-science simply never occurred. Risky business, this game of science.

But progress was being made between the first and sixteenth centuries A.D. in physics (largely D-science) and astronomy (largely P-science), which prepared the ground for the eventual resolution of the physics/astronomy problems by (among others) Galileo, Kepler, and Newton, and the integration of P-science with D-science by Bacon, Descartes, Galileo, and Newton. Nevertheless, those scientists of the middle ages were good soldiers in the army of science. They doggedly pursued their P-science or D-science "games," while the larger question — of how P-science and D-science would eventually fit together — remained disturbingly unresolved.

What is striking to us now as we look back at the long record of astronomy between Ptolemy and Galileo is how little the natural philosophers worried about the fact that their spheres lacked any sort of predictive force and how little the astronomers in their turn showed about the fact that their epicycles were incompatible with the

causal principles of the best physics of the day. It
is not as though the philosophers [early physicists
were known as natural philosophers] could have
been unaware that a true account of the causes
ought also be predictive, or that the astronomers
could have been indifferent to whether their
geometrical models represented real motions or
not. But each side bracketed the awkward
questions, and went about its own business, as
professionals are supposed to do. (McMullin,
1984, p. 48)

In astronomy during the seventeenth century, the
unification of prediction and explanation was accomplished in quick
successive steps by the work of Copernicus, Galileo, Kepler, and
finally, Newton. The enormity of this accomplishment, not only
for our understanding of planetary motion but also to signal the
dawn of a new type of integrated science, was not lost on citizens
of the eighteenth century. No less a literary figure than Alexander
Pope penned the following tribute to his contemporary:

Nature and nature's laws lay hidden in night:

God said, "Let Newton be!" and all was light.

And just what sort of a new integrated notion of science can be
found in Newtonian mechanics?

McMullin calls this new scientific ideal, T-science (for
Theoretical science) because it is theory-driven like the old
D-science. This new approach, however, also included
theory-driven predictions as an important part of the empirical
testing of the adequacy of any scientific theory. The new science
also worked backward from observed effects to possible (often
unseen) causes. These "putative causes" were called "theoretical
entities," which were then thought to bring about, explain, or cause
the observed effects. For example, an effect to be explained by the
theory of Newtonian mechanics might be a particular set of
planetary motions. Within Newtonian theory, gravity might be
postulated as the theoretical entity that causes the planets to move as
they do. It is the fact that the theory is capable of accurately
predicting known planetary motions, as well as its ability to predict
in advance the behavior of certain as yet unobserved phenomena
(such as comets), that underlies our belief in the validity of the
theory — and also represents the warrant for belief in the existence

of the theoretical entities (such as gravity) that populate the theory. Thus, we have a new ideal in science of explanation and prediction working in conjunction with one another.

Corrigible, testable theories lay at the heart of T-science. Scientific theories never contain Truth, as had been held in D-science approaches. But Truth remains an important part of T-science, not as an actually achievable goal, but as a never-reached, horizon-concept — the beacon toward which the scientist's efforts are directed. A theory now must make predictions, and testing now becomes a necessary part of science, as prediction represents the most important epistemic criterion (i.e., a scientist's best signal that his or her theory represents a step forward in the evolution of theories toward the Truth in this domain). Thus, prediction and explanation — which for so long had been separated — were now united.

So what now is our view of the ultimate aims and goals of T-science? Better theoretical understanding — pure and simple. And which theories represent our best guess as to what is the best understanding? The theory that best satisfies the epistemic criteria — pure and simple. But as Figure 1 suggests, predictive adequacy might be considered as the "first among equals" among epistemic criteria. Or at least I see it that way. For a more analytic treatment of the role of the epistemic criteria in theory choice see Kuhn (1977), McMullin (1983), and Howard (1985b).

Expanding upon our evolutionary metaphor, one can now understand the workings of T-science in the following manner. Science is the cauldron in which competing theoretical perspectives struggle for acceptance. Epistemic values function something like environmental presses in weeding out unfit theories in this competition. And predictive accuracy is now thought to be the most important of these criteria. While a theory might not be empirically adequate early in its development, any theory that does not eventually "square with the facts" will not long remain viable. It is an act of faith by scientists that if they keep their eyes firmly fixed upon the epistemic values (or, stated differently, theory choice should involve the judgmental application of the epistemic criteria), the resulting evolution of theories will represent ever-closer approximations to the Truth. The rules of thumb I suggested in Figure 1 can be considered as either "helpful hints" for scientists (as in the case of accuracy of measurement), or are implied by one of the epistemic values (since, e.g., falsifiability and testability are presupposed in predictive adequacy).

Goal

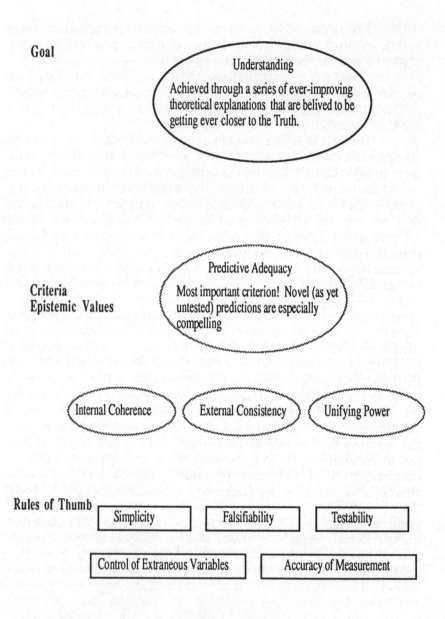

Understanding

Achieved through a series of ever-improving theoretical explanations that are belived to be getting ever closer to the Truth.

Criteria
Epistemic Values

Predictive Adequacy

Most important criterion! Novel (as yet untested) predictions are especially compelling

Internal Coherence   External Consistency   Unifying Power

Rules of Thumb

| Simplicity | Falsifiability | Testability |

| Control of Extraneous Variables | Accuracy of Measurement |

Figure 1: Ultimate goal, criteria, and rules of thumb in science.

My apologies! I've let this discussion get far too technical for the purposes of this book. Perhaps an analogy of science to a game like basketball will shed some light upon the way the epistemic criteria can guide scientists in their ultimate goal of improved understanding. Figure 2 presents a parallel breakdown of the ultimate goal, criteria for success, and helpful hints for a game of basketball.

When one asks a basketball coach what he or she hopes to do against a particular opponent, it would be a joke if he or she were to say "To have scored more points than our opponent by the end of the game." One simply does not state the ultimate goal of a game — that is taken for granted. Rather, coaches talk about what they need to do to "play good basketball," namely, play good offense, good defense, and rebound well. Being successful on these three criteria does not guarantee that one's team will win, but all coaches would be quite thrilled if they knew they would be successful on all three dimensions in a game. The helpful hints are just that — *generally* helpful hints. But one would not want to "involve all five players offensively" if one were employing some form of an isolation offense. The Chicago Bulls often try to isolate their best offensive player — Michael Jordan. The Boston Celtics from time to time play a "two-man game" on offense with Larry Bird and Kevin McHale being isolated on one side of the court in order to keep three of the defenders away from them. Similarly, the "Box out opponents on all shots" helpful hint might be counterindicated if, for example, one had a powerful front line and the coach wished to fast-break on offense. Guards are instructed not to box out when the opponents shoot, but instead to release immediately to initiate the fast break. This is a sink-or-swim strategy as it assumes your three best rebounders can out-rebound their five players (seriously jeopardizing the "rebound" criterion of good basketball). But, when successful, it can lead to some incredible high-probability shots, thus virtually assuring success on the "offensive" criterion. This strategy can make a good deal of sense when your opponent has an exceptionally strong defense because it can preempt an important strength the opponent typically exhibits.

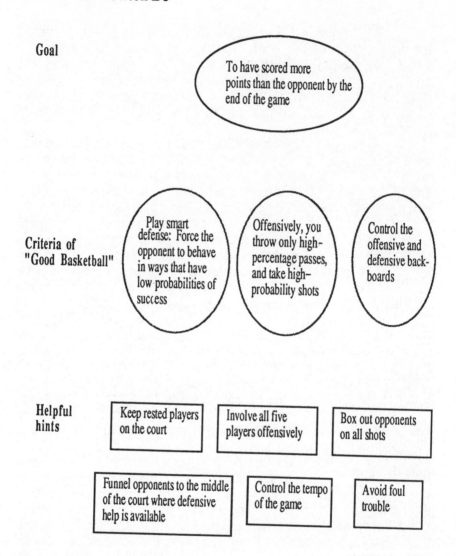

Figure 2: Ultimate goal, criteria, and helpful hints in basketball.

Similarly, working scientists frequently make strategic decisions regarding the implementation of the "helpful hints" of experimentation. For example, one can sometimes choose a certain experimental design that is less-than-perfect on the "accuracy of measurement" issue of the "cause" variable, because the design allows for a superb degree of control over extraneous variables. Every scientist knows that a good deal of tinkering with experimental procedures, design, equipment, and so forth is necessary before an experimental demonstration is ready to make its point. Does that make the interrelationships among the three levels of values in science any clearer?

Returning to the story of science in the seventeenth century, predictive accuracy became the most important criterion of good science. Thus, the most compelling scientific demonstrations were those where the scientist exhibited precise prediction and/or control over the phenomenon being studied (e.g., planetary motion, chemical reactions). But the Baconian revolution did more than integrate P-science and D-science into the new T-science; it also furnished an incredibly powerful example of how such a science might explain. Newton's mechanical universe represented a vivid picture of an elegant nonagentic, mechanical, scientific explanation. In the succeeding centuries, many thousands of scientists (consciously or unconsciously) sought to explain their phenomena of interest via elegant, mechanical explanations like Newton's. Having this vivid image of the "ideal scientific explanation" in mind proved helpful to many scientists in their efforts. But this vivid paradigm case of proper scientific explanation also kept other scientists from pursuing various types of explanations which were quite different in form from Newtonian mechanics.

Every creation reflects some characteristics of its creator. Since the rules of science were *not* a divine revelation but rather a human creation, its character might tell us something about the human mind. I believe it was Karl Popper who wondered, "What is the world that it can be known by the human mind? What is the mind that it can come to know the world?" But any creation also tells us something of that which it was created to do. I would like to consider some of the characteristics of science which resulted from the fact that our general notion of science evolved during the seventeenth century in response to breakthroughs in physics, astronomy, chemistry, optics, and so forth. To make my point somewhat differently, I'll ask a question. Would our notion of science now be different if the vision of T-science had been based upon consideration of accomplishments in psychology, political science, sociology, and economics? You can bet your telescope that it would have been different! But this is a difficult development to imagine, since we are asking how evolution would have proceeded in quite a different ecological niche — and then, we ask, would the set of superordinate principles (such as the criteria of scientific rationality mentioned in Figure 1) extracted from that hypothetical line of development have been the same (or different) from those that actually evolved? While this question might be virtually unanswerable, one might profitably reflect upon the notion of science that did develop, and how this general notion might be ill-fitting to the natures of certain entities, such as people, societies, economic systems, political groups, and so forth.

In Chapter 2 I promised to say more about Aristotle's four types of causes (or four different ways of understanding an action). They become important now, because the new T-science exhibited certain perspectives on causality (e.g., material, efficient) while simultaneously suggesting that science should *not* consider questions from other perspectives (e.g., final causality). A *material* cause is one that emanates from the substance or material of which a thing is made (e.g., glass is brittle because of the molecular structure of the material from which it is made). An *efficient* cause considers the impetus or force behind events, that is, the push, thrust, flow, or bringing-about elements in events. For example, when one billiard ball strikes another, it is the force of the first ball that is responsible for movement in the second ball. *Formal* cause depicts the pattern, shape, outline, or recognizable organization in the flow of events. Think of game plans or strategies in contests such as chess and football. As one watches a football game develop, the skilled observer might detect the coaches' game plans at odds with one another. Lastly, a *final* cause is that for the sake of which something occurs — the reason, purpose, intention, *telos* (end), or goal of events or actions. The final cause for my writing this book is to communicate to you some interesting possibilities that I see for a narrative or storytelling approach to human thought. Or, the final cause for your being on a diet might be for you to lose weight. Modern science, following the lead of Newtonian mechanics, became the search for material and efficient cause mechanisms responsible for any behavior in question. And how would scientists know which theories were more likely to be closer to the true mechanisms responsible for the behavior in question? The theories that enabled scientists to exhibit greater prediction and/or control (and the most impressive novel predictions that are later empirically confirmed) in their experiments were the most likely candidates.

Since the last few pages present what is a critical move for this entire book, it bears restating in a slightly different form. Please pardon what will be, I hope, a bit of helpful repetition. As a result of the Baconian revolution, the meaning of what constitutes properly scientific explanations (or the form a scientific explanation must take) underwent profound changes. Prior to the seventeenth century, scientists sometimes entertained telic explanations of phenomena, where anthropomorphization and agency were employed (i.e., the speed of a falling body being seen as a reflection of its "jubilation" upon approaching its proper place; species "intending" to evolve more effective defense mechanisms; etc.) But since the seventeenth century, *telic* explanations (directed toward an end; purposeful; final cause) increasingly have been excluded from the domain of scientific understanding. In fact, telic explanations are now frequently assumed to be prescientific, or amateurish efforts which eventually will be superceded by nonagentic, scientific explanations. Think back to the examples of explanations given at the beginning of Chapter 2. You remember: quarreling gods producing thunder; jubilant rocks falling quickly while ambivalent feathers fall more slowly. Those accounts couldn't have been properly scientific explanations since they did not highlight the *nonagentic material and/or efficient cause mechanisms responsible for the observed effects.* They appealed to final cause influence, and thus would be problematic to the scientific ear, whether the performing agent was a god, a rock, or a person. That is the reason one would today find such explanations "fishy sounding" even though one might not have a clue as to how, for example, thunder is produced.

Now think about a creation reflecting the nature of *that for which it was created.* I would like to argue that for the subject matters of interest for the sciences that developed during the seventeenth and eighteenth centuries (i.e., planets in astronomy; gravitational attraction in physics; chemical reactions in chemistry, etc.) *nontelic explanations are most appropriate,* and final cause or telic accounts are generally wrongheaded. But perhaps the opposite is close to being true for the study of human beings in psychology. Unfortunately, I'm jumping far ahead in my story. Chapters 8 through 13 will consider what a scientific psychology that includes telic, final cause explanations might look like. But before we consider a fully human science — not just one that attempts to adopt (and modify slightly) the research methods of the established natural sciences — we must trace the development of psychology in its first century as an empirical study of human action. Tracing the early development of the science of psychology will be done in Chapter 6.

Finally, the development of the natural sciences from the eighteenth century to the present (while fascinating in its own right) has little import for the purposes I have in telling this particular story of science. Thus, I'll only make one additional observation. In some respects, the notion of prediction in science, and its relationship to theory development, seemed somewhat clearer in the eighteenth century than it does today. For example, the predictive accuracy of theories in cosmology (such as the Big Bang theory) is somewhat troublesome. Surely, one would *not* want to require a cosmological theory to exhibit predictive characteristics for other universes than our own. Instead, such theories make rather esoteric predictions which often only a specialist in that field can see as exhibiting support for one theory rather than another. Similarly, our experience of the quantum world suggests that exact prediction of the behavior of entities like electrons might represent an inappropriate ambition. In short, modern science has run up against certain situations where the naive belief — that scientific theories make predictions about the actions of entities, and the scientist then checks the accuracy of these predictions — is clearly insufficient. Yet we have found that science can still proceed if we judiciously modify and adapt our understanding of the meaning of the criterion of predictive accuracy to the particular characteristics of the objects of interest (e.g., the worlds of the infinitesimally small and almost infinitely large). Thus, while the role of predictive accuracy in modern science is less straightforward than it was three hundred years ago, it still represents the most important criterion value in science. So the seventeenth century did not mark the end of new insights into the nature of scientific rationality, just the turning point. The adventure continues even to this day.

Chapter 5

My Life as Seen by Others

An acorn never falls very far from the tree.

—Everybody says it

You can't really understand me unless you have a feel for my parents. Thus, I wanted them to give their perspectives on my life story. But since they aren't professional writers, they are reluctant to write anything that might show up in a book. Besides, they are as paranoid of the probing and questioning of a psychologist (any psychologist!) as are the rest of you. So I had to have a plausible cover story to get them talking. I told them that I had no memory of anything that happened to me prior to kindergarten (which is true!). Thus, I indicated that I wanted them to tell some stories of me as a very young child. Knowing my parents, I knew that once they started talking, their comments would range over broader spans of my life. At their request, the interviews were conducted with each parent separately, and lasted about forty-five minutes each. I had written Chapters 1, 3, and 7 before the interviews, and my parents read them for the first time immediately after their interviews. I have omitted those comments that were irrelevant to the themes being traced in the *Story of George*. Further, the sequence of statements in the text is often different from the order in which they were told to me. I have edited their text only lightly in order to keep the flavor of how they made their points. For this entire chapter, anything in bold type represents either a question I asked of them or a clarification I entered into their comments. I brought my parents into this project for several reasons: I am tremendously proud of them; I want you to get to know them better; I believe their perspective on my life will enrich your understanding of my story; and as any author knows, if you can get someone else to write a chapter for you — but you don't share royalties with them — you go for it!

Let's start with an event early in my life that

both Mom and Dad brought up. You might get a sense for their differing storytelling styles by comparing their versions of my first pugilistic success — I knocked my father out at age three!

Dad: "You were a very nice, easygoing baby. As nice as you'd want to see. We could do most anything with you. You played by yourself, with other kids, and you were very content with just any little toy. One day you came out to see what I was doing in the yard, and I was digging a post hole for a new fence. There was a rock in the bottom of it and I was laying down trying to pull the rock out and I had a two-by-four as a tamping pole leaning up against a tree and I didn't see you or know you were around. When I came to, I found out later that you had come out to see what I was doing and touched this two-by-four and it fell and konked me on the head and knocked me out and that was the end of the pole digging for that day. But you were too young to realize what you were doing."

Mom: "One day when Dad was starting to build a fence between our place and McDerby's, he had posts dipped in creosote and he was trying to make a hole for them down far enough to be stable, and you wanted to get out with him. You promised that you wouldn't get in the way, that you would just watch him. So I dressed you and I let you go out. Your favorite position was leaning against a big tree in the back yard so when Dad was down to his armpit trying to get out a big rock that was in the hole, and he was digging around it and he was down with his hands in the hole, which left his head laying in the hole, you got over to look at him and you decided to lean. Instead of leaning against the tree you leaned against the post which was standing against the tree and it went Pow! Knocked Dad in the back of the head and he really passed out for a minute or two. Well, when you came in I said, 'thought you wanted to go out and watch Dad' and you said, 'Yeah, but he went to sleep in the hole.' I went to the window just in time to see him become conscious holding the back of his head saying 'Oooohhhh!' So I sent you up to Grandma's."

How about another story they both recalled? Let mom speak first this time.

Mom: "One time Grandma was helping you practice your spelling, and you said, 'We had the most interesting class on Friday afternoon. We learned all about testicles.' Grandma said, 'Oh my God, I don't believe that. Those nuns have gone too far — what they're now teaching children! What did you learn about testicles?' You said, 'Well, I learned that everybody has two.'

And Grandma says, 'No dear, just boys and men.' You said, 'No Grandma, everybody in the world has two.' And Grandma says, 'No, George, you have to learn this right. Only men and boys have testicles.' So Bocky says, 'Mom, please leave him alone.' And Grandma says, 'Why would Sister tell him that?' Bocky says, 'Maybe Sister's got a set?' So Grandma says, 'What else did you learn?' You said, 'Well you have one larger one and one smaller one.' And Grandma says, 'Now I'm the age I am, and I never heard that one before. And what else did you learn?' You said, 'And your food passes through them.' Grandma shouts, 'Glory be to God, I never knew that!' So Billy, who is in the first grade, sticks his head out from under the table, where he had been playing solitaire, 'Hey, George, isn't that your intestines?' And you said, 'Oh yeah! Sorry, I always get them mixed up.'

Dad: "In your younger days when you were first going to school, it was Sis and I tutoring you all of the time and giving you time constantly and it all started about the second grade and we spent hours with you. One day we were tutoring you and you came up with a quote that your teacher said that all your food passes through your testicles and you had two of them — a large one and a small one. Well, your grandmother was sitting near the table and she heard you and she said, 'As old as I am I never heard that before.' Billy was playing under the table and out of the clear blue sky he pipes out, 'George, that ain't testicles that's your intestines.'

About this idyllic childhood I painted in Chapter 1 — how does Dad see it?

Dad: "You were a very nice child. Easy to get along with. When you boys were about three and one and a half, I was wrestling on the floor with you and Billy was about to fall, so I kind of rolled over to protect him, and my knee hit you on the chin. After it was over you said, 'Daddy, is we having fun?' I don't know what you call fun, but I felt very sorry for you. That's the way you were — just a very quiet boy. We had a family next door with three boys and a little girl about your age. You all played together constantly and you all got along very nicely. In one house or the other, whoever was home was where the group was allowed to play. You had very good relations with all of the kids on the street except one. There was one kid on the block named Paul who was a hyper kid. He would come out and want to play with you and then you would start playing, and you wouldn't be together but a very few minutes before he would haul off and let you have one — and then run home. This happened so many times. Your grandmother was there one day right after this happened and promised you a penny if you would beat Paul up. So for a penny, you would do most anything. That was like a hundred dollars to you. You sailed into Paul and gave him all that he needed. But other than that, that was about the extent of the fighting. You were a very nice boy.

"About the same time, school was going on and you got through kindergarten fine, and first grade was great. Starting about the second grade you started having difficulties. We practically had to drum everything into you. You just didn't seem to grasp anything. But you were always willing — you wanted to do it. So after a couple of years like this — things did improve some. Then you were getting to the age of Little League. And other things came into your life. Before that, the kids played stickball on the street. You were the most competitive boy I ever seen. You wanted to win at all costs — but yet in a very mild-mannered way. If one of the kids on your team wasn't trying hard, you would come in crying because they wouldn't play hard. But no fights or arguments or nothing about it. But you just wanted to win, just like in your studies at school you would just stay with 'em constantly until you got the work done. The further on you went in life, it seemed like, the easier things got. You worked and played as hard as you could."

George: How about my workaholic ways? How far back do they go? And where might they have come from?

Dad: "When you were in Little League and in school, your schoolwork seemed like it was getting better. You seemed to be getting the grasp of doing it. Though at times you had to put in a lot of hours — but very willingly. No one had to tell you to put the time in. You just did it automatically. You went into high school at Marist, a Catholic high school, and you were very much the same. You practiced your sports very hard. You'd come home bushed, but still had to do your studies. And you'd work 'til you couldn't stay awake anymore. Because of my work, I had to get up early in the morning. You'd tell me to call you when I got up. This is one of the unreal things about you, I didn't think any kid could do it. I would call you in the morning, you'd come right downstairs, sit down at the table, and start your homework. You wouldn't go to the bathroom to relieve yourself, you wouldn't go to wash the sleep out of your eyes; you'd just pick up your homework and go at it. How you did it, I don't know. But you would do this day in and day out. And it seemed to work. [To

this day, my best work gets done early in the morning—long before anyone else arrives at the office.]
"You got everything going for yourself, the higher you got in school the easier it was for you. When you finished Marist High School, you decided to go into the novitiate. Well, that was your decision. Your mother and I talked it out and decided 'Well, if that's what he wants we'll let him go.' So, then we lost touch with you to a certain extent because we were allowed to visit you very infrequently. You weren't allowed to come home. So it was, that you grew up on your own. We couldn't do much about it. When you came out of Marist College, and you're home here a while, oh, I guess a month or more, and this discussion came up. We knew that you passed your courses at college. But in the discussion you said, 'Well, I finished college *cum laude*.' Your mother and I had never heard this, or never seen anything to that effect, and so we doubted it. You went and brought out your transcript and it was right on there. So, we had lost you, as far as closeness, to the extent that you wanted to serve the brothers for a while even after you had come out of the order. You had notified them that you didn't want to be a brother. But while you were going to the novitiate, you were very aggressive not only in your studies but you also did everything that was possible for the novitiate. You ran different programs for the novitiate. You ran summer programs for ghetto kids from Newberg and Kingston, New York. **[God, if I ever need a press agent, I know where I can get a good one — cheap!]**
"The brothers had this summer camp in New Hampshire, and they had a very, very bad winter up there. The snow was tremendously deep and it caved in any number of their barracks for this summer camp. So, when it came time for the summer camp, you asked me if I would take a week's vacation and go up and help rebuild these camp barracks. I agreed to take a week's vacation and go up. Well, I never worked so hard in my life. **[He says with glee in his eyes!]** We went to work repairing the barracks. There were any number of brothers working. They paired me up with an old brother that I think was seventy-one years old at the time. We were laying flooring as the other brothers built the barracks. I tell you, that old man could really go. If you kept up with him, you knew you had done a good day's work. But it was the same way with all of those brothers. I never saw men work like they did on those buildings. They had an outside contractor working the other side of the camp. He was doing the same type of work on other barracks. These brothers would just go right by

them — they had about the same amount of men and we would start at 8 o'clock and work until 11 o'clock. The contractor's men worked until noon.

We had a happy hour before lunch — *that* I enjoyed. But then at 1 o'clock it was back to work and the same thing in the evening — we had our happy hour. We knocked off early and had our happy hour and those other fellas were still working for the contractor and our work was progressing much faster. The contractor said, 'If I had a bunch of men in a novitiate working for me, I'd be a rich man in a few years.' He said he never saw men work like those brothers did, and if you kept up with them you knew that you did a day's work."

My parents always taught us that in the final analysis each of us was responsible for the lives we'd live. Thus, we made our own decisions and my parents stood by our decisions, even when they disagreed.

George: "Let me remind you of something that maybe you forgot. When I graduated from high school, you went to my graduation. When it was all over, and we were walking away, you put your arm around me and said, 'Boy, I'm right proud of you. I never thought you were going to make it.'**

Dad: "I forgot all about that."

George: "Well, tell us what you were thinking."

Dad: "That was the high school days. Well, when you finished high school and graduated, well, I had to congratulate you so I put my arm around you and told you, 'Boy, you made it. But I'll tell you it was sweat, tears, and everything — but you made it through.' And it was more on your pluck and desire, and maybe the encouragement that your mother and I gave you. But it seemed like the higher you got in school work, the easier the whole thing came to you. You put in a lot of hours, that very few kids would ever do, to accomplish what you did, and we're proud of you for that. You did very nicely. And I think that's all I'm going to talk about."

Sure, Dad! Thanks for the stories. What about my mom's recollections of my childhood?

George: "What about my school?"

Mom: "OK! You remember when you were in kindergarten and your big job was that you had a dustpan and brush and you were supposed to get the dust under the radiators every morning. After which Sister Eimard would open her little box of crystal hardtack candy and you were allowed to take a piece.

One morning you went over and said 'Sister, may I have my piece of candy first and while it's in my mouth I will keep my mouth closed and I won't be getting all that dust in my mouth?' Sister had said the candy was to take the dust out of your mouth, but you thought it would be a good idea if you could have it first."

George: "What about everybody living together on 12th Street: Nanna, Bocky, the McDerbys, Bub, us?"

Mom: "In the same neighborhood. Well, everybody knew the rules. When the McDerbys came into my house, they sat on the floor, watched television, played games, they took off their shoes and walked around in their socks. When you kids went to the McDerbys house you ran a bit wild, jumped on the furniture, everything. There were easier rules at the McDerbys. Grandma McDerby noticed this once, and she mentioned it to me. And it was the truth. The McDerbys jumped on their beds and on their furniture and so you people went right along with them. But when they came in our house, they lived by our laws."

George: "What are your recollections about my deciding to go into the Marist novitiate?"

Mom: "Oh, I felt bad. *And*, I felt caught. I had Father Darcy over here one night for supper and I was complaining that I wanted you to go to college, or to go out and work for a few years, until you were twenty-one. And I mentioned that I wanted you to get out of the Marists' sphere of influence for a while. And Father Darcy hopped all over me, saying that if I didn't want you in the Marists' sphere of influence, why did I send you to Marist High School in the first place? And you were upset with me, too. I remember you stood there and said, 'Mom, if you're wondering if I'm mature, let me tell you that I'm emotionally mature, and I'm sexually mature!' And I said, 'Oh! I'm glad to hear that because you father is fifty-two and he's neither!' [I remember that my father and mother thought that was *very* funny. Father Darcy and I didn't — as it was our ox taking the goring.] Dad was the one who thought of this — he said 'Sis, he may go in and stay, or he may come out. But at least he's in a safe place, and he's heading in the right direction.' This from the Protestant! And so I felt alright about it.

"Now one thing that I remember is that you always wanted a set of rules — you were just happier if you knew what you could expect to happen. Remember? It would be a Friday night and Lil [my mother's sister] would be over with her kids, and Peggy [our neighbor Peggy McDerby] would be over with her kids, and you'd be playing or there'd be some great ballgame on TV. Now the normal, weekday schedule would be: 7 o'clock it was time for baths; you'd be in bed by 7:30 — usually; and asleep, hopefully, at 8. If it was a Friday night and you didn't realize that you didn't have school the next day, you would come over (and this was when you were very small — like six or seven years old) and tap me on the leg and say, 'Mom, shouldn't you be getting us ready for bed now?' And I had to explain that there was no school tomorrow, and you could stay in bed a little later. And you would say, 'Oh! OK!' You would be joyous, but you would certainly have left the game in order to keep the rule. That kept up a long time. Remember when you were in the novitiate, when you came down to Marion's wedding. Brother Bill and Brother Martin were your superiors then, and they came with you. And you people were supposed to be home to the novitiate by midnight. Do you remember what kept happening at the wedding reception? You, me, Father Hart, and the two Brothers were sitting together and you kept reaching over and saying to Brother Bill 'It's 10:30 now, shouldn't we be starting back?' and he'd say 'Yes, I know, George.' And in a little while you'd say 'Brother, it's twenty 'til eleven.' And finally Father Hart said, 'Oh, George, for goodness sake, relax. It's your sister's wedding — and these guys *are your superiors*!' He couldn't believe that you were that worried about breaking the rules."

George: "I was just a rookie monk then."

Mom: "You were just a coward! You didn't want to break a rule.

"I didn't like you being in the novitiate at that time. Being isolated from the outside world, not being able to write letters or read newspapers, or watch TV, that kind of stuff I did not like. I also remember thinking how easy it was for your father when we were leaving after one of those 'visitation' afternoons. All he does is hop in the car and think about driving, while I'm there in the back seat just dried-out, wet-out, whatever — I can't even think or talk — there's a lump in my throat, everything. And Dad makes the wrong turn getting off the novitiate property. And Marion said, 'Dad! What's the matter with you? That's not the way to go. You made a wrong turn.' And he said, 'Oh, I'm sorry, but my eyes are a little misty.'

"Oh, by the way, did I ever tell you? The day you went to the novitiate, I went into the bedroom you and Billy shared and I dismantled your bed. Remember? You had twin beds. I dismantled it because I just couldn't bear to see your empty bed every morning when I'd have to make up Billy's bed."

George: "Dad, how did you feel about my going into the novitiate?"

Dad: "Personally, I didn't like it and I don't think your mother did either. But it was your decision so we went along with it."

George: "What didn't you like about it? Could you be more specific?"

Dad: "Well, what we didn't like about it was that we were losing you as a son. You were going into an altogether foreign country as far as we were concerned. Someone else was taking our place. It really went against our grain, but you can hang onto a person for only so long, and so we decided to let you go and see if that was what you wanted. We tried to be as strong-minded as possible. And at the same time your older sister was giving us some problems. She wanted to go into the Peace Corps and go to Africa. At that time Africa wasn't a safe place to go. We finally got her to go to a mission in Texas, if that's what she wanted. We were relieved when she decided to go to a place in this country. So she ended up with some order of nuns down in Texas, working with the underprivileged Mexican farm help. She was teaching them English in school. So we felt better about her being there — but it was that we were losing our children faster than we wanted to. But it all worked out for the best. You all did what you wanted."

George: "Leave it to Mom to always have one last story."

Mom: "Oh! Another thing I just remembered, when you were on the basketball team in high school, and a game was going against you people, you committed your last foul and had to come out of the game. And everybody was saying it was a rotten call and you were really upset at the referee. I was watching your face and I thought 'Oh no! That's the look he gets when he's about to cry.' So, it was a quiet part of the game while the guy was getting ready to shoot his foul shot, and so I stood up, cupped my hands around my mouth, and yelled, 'That's alright Georgie — it's only a game.' Your coach, Knoblach, turned beet red and turned around and yelled 'It is *not* only a game!' Do you remember that?"

George: "Only vaguely! Sometimes repression can be great. But I feel good that you helped me to know the difference between what's really important in life, and what's just a game." *As always*, Mom has the last word.

George: "Mom, you're telling very positive stories about me. And I wasn't perfect, there must be some stories you could. . ."

Mom (interrupting): "I told you, you had colic for the first six weeks of your life and you did nothing but cry morning, noon, and night."

George: "And I was perfect from then on?"

Mom: "I can't— Maybe it's my point of view, from where I'm now standing, but I can't remember anything negative. I really can't. Now turn that off!"

So much for a balanced picture. Well, at least I tried.

Chapter 6

Humans Are Important Entities!
Let's Study Them Scientifically

In the last analysis, man has only his future. Even
the purposes to which he will put the past, are part
of his future. On the sands of time not one footprint
can be erased, but the future is open country. Within
the unknowable final limits of human nature, we
shall go where we please, as far as we choose to see.
The ultimate function of prophecy is not to tell the
future, but to make it.

— W. W. Wager

The remarkable scientific breakthroughs and subsequent
technological wonders that took place in the natural sciences
between the seventeenth and nineteenth centuries greatly enhanced
the status of science in the minds of most people. During that time,
science went from being "one of several possible approaches to
gaining knowledge" to being (in the minds of many) "the best
possible method for arriving at veridical answers to questions about
the world." The *scientific method* was often ballyhooed as an
all-purpose technique, ready-made to crank out the truth about a
question in almost any domain. Extending the scientific method to
new domains (e.g., economics, sociology, etc.) was a prime task
for nineteenth-century scholars. And as the title of this chapter
suggests, it was inevitable that the seemingly all-purpose
knowledge-producing machine of science would be turned upon the
most important and most perplexing of all entities — human beings
themselves. Remarkably, it was about a dozen years before the
advent of the twentieth century that a sustained attempt at the
scientific study of humans was finally undertaken. Thus, scientific
psychology is barely one hundred years old — just a kid, as
sciences go.

Right from the start there was enormous controversy in
psychology regarding the goals (see Chapter 2) of a scientific study
of humans and the forms (see Chapter 4) of explanations of human
action that should be entertained. Willhelm Wundt envisioned two
types of psychology: A natural science type (*Naturwissenschaft*),

and a folk psychology that borrowed from studies in the humanities (*Geisteswissenschaft*). For a brief time it looked as if this dual approach to human action might persist, and two strains of scientific psychology (like Babylonian P-science and Greek D-science) might emerge. But to make a very long and complex story "short and sweet," it didn't turn out that way. Unfortunately, the natural science approach urged by progenitors like John B. Watson won out, and relegated a human science perspective to the status of an outcast. Thus, while descendants of the early folk psychology such as humanistic psychology, gestalt psychology, phenomenological psychology, ethnomethodology, and psychobiography still flourish, they have exerted very little influence on the course of *scientific psychology*.

Scientific psychology in the image of the natural sciences (namely, looking *only* for material cause and efficient cause explanations of human action) assumed ascendancy. Consider Watson's (1925) extremist rhetoric: "psychology, as the behaviorist views it, is a pure, objective, experimental branch of natural science which needs consciousness as little as do the sciences of chemistry and physics." I'm sure part of you recoils from that statement, and exclaims something like, "Be serious Professor Watson, a complete and accurate explanation of human action that completely ignores the role of human consciousness? Impossible!" While I think you are completely correct in your disbelief that such a restrictive scientific analysis of human action is even possible, we must appreciate the dilemma in which Watson and other early research psychologists found themselves.

Psychologists whose lives straddled both the nineteenth and twentieth centuries thought they knew what it meant to give a "scientific explanation." It was a nonagentic, mechanistic explanation that focused upon material and efficient cause explanations of human action. And while many of the leaders in the field (such as Wundt and William James) believed that an understanding of humans limited to the natural science model would fail to capture important aspects of humans (i.e., consciousness, free will, values, language, etc.), *they were unsuccessful in articulating a compelling, alternative research-based understanding* — namely an appropriate human science. Misgivings to the contrary, pro natural science rhetoric like Watson's (1925), "If 'mind' acts on body, then all physical laws are invalid," won the day. Reinforced by the tremendous influence of Logical Positivism on psychology in the 1930s, 1940s, and 1950s, scientific psychology became virtually identical with a natural science approach (looking for material and efficient cause influences in human action) to human action.

Since the story of the first hundred years of mainstream scientific psychology is well known, I will not completely flesh out that tale here. Rather, readers who wish to examine the story of scientific psychology's first century are directed toward Koch and Leary's (1985) excellent *A Century of Psychology as Science.* In reviewing the history of one basic area of psychological research after another (e.g., sensory processes, perception, learning, motivation, emotion, cognition, development, personality, and social) a similar theme emerges remarkably often. The theme involves early enthusiasm with the prospects for a scientific analysis of each area of psychological study. This optimism is then followed by important research-based insights in each of these domains. Quickly thinkers begin to explore the inevitable limitations of a narrowly scientific view of human action. And, finally, they express the hope that in the next hundred years as a science their field will not only see expanded and appropriate new perspectives and methodologies, but also that these changes will somehow lead to a more compelling and integrated view of human action.

Good scientists are always open to better ways of studying their subject matters. It falls to advocates of human science perspectives to develop and defend appropriate ways of understanding human action properly. The first book in this trilogy, *Dare We Develop a Human Science*, highlighted why self-determination must be part of a complete understanding of humans. This book broadens that basic theme, and suggests that storytelling might be the basic mechanism whereby people structure their lives and actions, and thereby achieve the power of directing their lives. But before I leave "psychology conceived solely as a natural science," I must emphasize two important points. First, there are important material cause and efficient cause influences on human behavior, and any complete account of human action *must* clarify the cause and effect relationships of these types at work. Our inaugural century as a science has returned handsome dividends in understanding the material and efficient cause nature of human action. Second, an enormous amount was also learned about how properly to conduct research with humans (e.g., measurement theory, experimental and quasi-experimental design, statistical analysis, and much more). Because of the lessons learned from our natural science psychology experience, conceptually and methodologically speaking, we are now in a far better position to develop a human science approach to human action than were our forebears such as Wundt and James. I would argue that our case of "physics-envy" was not a complete disaster, but rather furnished us with some hard-won, valuable lessons that will make us better scientists in the future.

Lest you get the impression that the human science approach was completely abandoned to the natural science perspective, I should indicate that the alternative tradition remained alive and can be traced from Willhelm Wundt (1832 - 1920), Franz Brentano (1838 - 1917), and William James (1842 - 1910) through Gordon Allport (1897 - 1967), Abraham Maslow (1908 - 1970), and George Kelly (1905 - 1967) to contemporaries such as Carl Rogers (1902 - 1987), Henry Murray (1893 -   ) and Joseph Rychlak (1928 -   ). Further, psychologists who have had to deal with people in applied ways, such as clinicians, counselors, educational psychologists, industrial/organizational psychologists, and so forth, have always understood people as conscious, intending, active agents who were not merely mechanistically responding to material and efficient causal influences upon them. Instead, applied psychologists have always known that people are constantly striving to achieve ends in their lives — to make something of their time on earth. Or as Carl Jung claimed in a 1984 BBC interview, "Man cannot stand a meaningless life." But how does one conduct rigorous scientific studies of meaningfulness? The problem is clear to research psychologists, but for many years, no clear solutions emerged. But the fact that scientific psychologists hold mechanistic models of humans while practitioners generally view their clients as somewhat self-determining active agents is frequently cited as a major reason for the deep and bitter scientist-practitioner schism that plagues the discipline to this day. The problem is so acute that civil war between scientists and practitioners has broken out within the discipline's central organization, the American Psychological Association, with the scientifically oriented faction moving toward secession.

Let me try an example of a simple everyday behavior — jogging — to demonstrate the dilemma that scientific psychology — viewed solely as a natural science — faces. As you'll see in Chapter 10, for several years I didn't exercise regularly, and now I take brisk walks and/or jog regularly. One might reasonably ask, "Why does George now jog?"

Well, one could explain my desire to exercise daily as being due to my becoming gradually addicted to my own endorphines (i.e., naturally occurring brain opiates). This is a nice, material cause explanation. The jogging could also be seen as performing a maintenance function in my family system — perhaps my spouse and children lavish praise upon me for exercising regularly. This represents an example of how social pressure might serve as an efficient cause "push" to get me to act in a certain way. To this point, psychology conceived solely as a natural science would have no problem with my analysis of my jogging. That is, a John B. Watson-type would acknowledge that endorphins and social pressure could represent proper factors in a scientific explanation of human action. But suppose you were to ask me about my jogging, and I was to say, "Lately I've been thinking that I might have a heart attack — and perhaps even die. I'm exercising regularly now to give myself every chance I can to avoid a coronary." Well, this is obviously a telic (or final cause) explanation, and thus is suspect as a scientific explanation — from the natural science perspective. When you mention your reservation about telic explanations, I say that I've experienced some chest pains on my left side of late, and so I got a check-up. The physician said one cholesterol reading (the one associated with eating fatty foods) was fine. But she also indicated that the "good cholesterol" reading was too low. She said I needed to exercise regularly. She also believed there was too much stress in my life, and that I should reduce that stress. I thought it over and decided I would try to get someone to serve as chair of the psychology department. I told my dean that one term as chair would be all I'd like to do, and he said, "Fine! Find somebody to take your place." And ever since Naomi Meara agreed to serve the department as chairperson, I don't feel nearly as stressed as I once did.

Doesn't that sound to you like a really good explanation of why I am now exercising regularly? Yet if you were a scientific psychologist, you might now have a queasy feeling in the pit of your stomach. In its first century as science, psychology never developed a way of including such final cause (or agent causality) factors in its explanations. Our model of science simply was incapable of appreciating some of the characteristics of human beings. Instead of first analyzing the characteristics of humans (such as agency) and then imagining a science capable of appreciating these human capacities, we tried to squeeze all of human functioning into the kinds of causality that were successful in explaining the behavior of inanimate and insentient entities.

Finally, there has long been an unfilled void in the hearts of many scientific psychologists. Stated simply, we have moved from a time of "grand theories" (such as the Freudian psychoanalytic approach, the learning theories of the 1950s, etc.) in psychology to "mini-theories" (e.g., need for achievement, social desirability responding, etc.). Further, like all sciences, our research has become evermore fragmented and specialized. Thus, it is increasingly difficult to see how new findings fit into the larger picture of human action. And perhaps most disturbing of all, I believe that the nature of the "big picture" in psychology is now greatly different from the ambitions that energized the founding fathers — whether of the natural scientific or human scientific stripe — to launch their great adventure into the scientific study of humans — a New Psychology. But psychology has conveniently — and unfortunately — forgotten the original ambitions of the founding fathers of the discipline. Such pillars of the science of psychology as G. Stanley Hall, Raymond B. Cattell, and William James chose to pursue vocations in psychology because "the New Psychology offered them an opportunity to resolve personal conflicts concerning science and religion, materialism and spiritualism, determinism and free will" (Leary, 1987, p. 316). But the science they founded has thus far contributed next to nothing toward the resolution of these ancient problems. The trajectory of psychology's development has largely precluded direct, serious consideration of these eternal conundra because we simply knew of no way that the issues could be investigated experimentally. Thus, research psychologists have been forced to turn from important, eternal questions of human nature to a variety of less critical — but infinitely more tractable — research issues.

But there is reason for new hope. In just the past three years a methodology for isolating and quantifying the proportion of human action in a particular domain caused by self-determination (a final cause explanation) has been developed (see Howard & Conway, 1986). Hooray! That's a step in the right direction. Even more exciting, in the past year it has been shown experimentally that a person's ability to self-determine in a particular domain is strongly influenced by the *meaningfulness* of the action for the person (see Howard, Curtin & Johnson, 1988). [Think about it! I can't make myself exercise. . . I get chest pains . . . My doctor says the test suggests I haven't been exercising enough. . . Does exercise become more meaningful to me?. . . Be serious!. . . And lo and behold a miracle occurs. . . I now can exercise at will!] Well, to make the entire story even more interesting, many theoreticians (not to mention many thousands of practitioners) are claiming that people think in *stories* (see Mair,

1977; Sarbin, 1986; Polkinghorne, 1988). So the meaningfulness of things is a function of their place in their story. And here I sit with a book on the narrative or storytelling approach to psychology half-written! Boy, did I get lucky — or what? But I'm getting a bit ahead of my story of science. Chapter 8 will detail the steps toward a human science of psychology more fully. But before that, we have one more installment in the *Story of George* saga.

Chapter 7

Quo Vadis? (Where Are You Going?)

I've seen many tragedies in my life. Fortunately,
most of them never occurred.

— Mark Twain

It was a very strange symposium at the 1986 American Psychological Association convention. Strange because there was no designated topic. So I asked the chairwoman of the session, "What should I talk about? " She said, "Just tell us exactly what you will do for the rest of your career. Make a prophecy!" So here's what I said:

The title of this talk is *Quo Vadis?* — or Where are you going? Well, I'm not at all comfortable in the role of the prophet — and here's the reason why:

If twenty years ago someone had asked me to predict what career I would be involved in in 1986, the term *psychology* would definitely not even have been mentioned.

If ten years ago I'd attempted to foresee my work of the next decade, the term *research* probably would have appeared only in the following context, "Since I've *finally* finished my dissertation 'research,' I can get on to what I really want to do. . ."

And lastly, if a short five years ago I'd played the role of the futurist, the word *freedom* might have slipped into my account only in passing, something like, "Once I get tenure I'll finally have the *freedom* to conduct research on really important issues."
Psychology — Research — Freedom

So now I'm going to tell you that for the remaining years of my career I intend to — you guessed it — Conduct *Research* on the *Psychology* of Personal *Freedom*!

Now let me be clear about what I'm asserting in seriousness: I do intend to conduct research on the psychology of free will (or self-determination, or personal causation, or volition or agency) or whatever you want to call that human capacity. What I am not taking too seriously is my ability (or anyone else's) accurately to predict the future.

But if I don't believe in people's ability accurately to predict the future, how can I believe in their capacity to be self-determining, willful, or volitional? Let me approach an answer by analogy: I sometimes think of myself as if I were a fish! [I'd like to picture myself as a twenty-five-inch rainbow trout — but an eight-inch sucker might be closer to the truth.] So here I am in this stream of life, and I think: "I could burrow into the mud today" or "Maybe I'll lie under that log for awhile" or "Perhaps I'll swim upstream and see what's happening." Well, one might say I'm self-determining — right? But we know that events — like whether or not a worm gets washed downstream or a fly lands on the surface of the stream — are really important considerations in what a fish will eventually do. Whether or not those potential dinners are imbedded with hooks could be of more than minor import upon our finny friends' life course. And we fish don't even like to think about the possibility of apocalyptic events like droughts, acid rain, floods, hydroelectric plants, chemical spills, and the like. So you can see why it is problematic — even for our self-determining fish — to predict his or her life course.

While analogies are very important for science, it is crucial to know where analogies fail. For example, call me a speciesist, but I doubt that any fish in history ever thought the following: "I wonder by what methodology one could rationally partition the variance in a particular behavior attributable to self-determination from the variance caused by biological factors, psychic determination, environmental influences, social pressures, and the like?" However, I can guarantee that at least one human being in this room (me!) seriously considered that thorny problem. So humans are different from fish in some important ways. But fishy models of human behavior are not overrunning psychology. (Pardon me, I meant to say: But *fish* models of human behavior are not overrunning psychology.) We employ other kinds of models: hydraulic analogies, reinforcement maximization machine models, and perhaps most commonly — computer analogies.

By the way, have you heard Gregory Bateson's comment upon the computer analogy of human behavior? Well here it is:

> A man wanted to know about mind, not in nature, but in his private large computer. He asked it (no doubt in his best Fortran), "Do you compute that you will ever think like a human being?" The machine then set to work to analyze its own computational habits. Finally, the machine printed its answer on a piece of paper, as such machines do. The man ran to get the answer and found, neatly typed, the words: THAT REMINDS ME OF A STORY.

Well, like all of you, I've been telling myself a story about my professional life — the most recent line of which you've already heard, "*I intend to conduct research on the psychology of personal freedom.*" Let me pull together these rambling thoughts by telling you a few things about *my story*.

Many of you remember Vince Harren. Vince was the director of the counseling psychology program at Southern Illinois University when I was a graduate student there. Vince was a humanistic psychologist; a wonderful human being; and a good friend. I, on the other hand, was a semi-serious graduate student who was hell-bent on getting out of what I perceived to be silly course requirements. On one occasion I went to Vince's office and had the following conversation: "Vince, I can't stand another semester of psychological assessment. Would you please waive that requirement of a second semester?" To my utter amazement Vince winked at me and said, "Sure George, a course in assessment really isn't important *for the person who is going to make research in humanistic psychology respectable!*"

My mind was racing with thoughts like "You've got to be out of your mind. . . There isn't a snowball's chance in hell that I'd. . . *You're* the humanistic psychologist, Vince, not me. . . I don't think humanistic research can *ever* be made respectable."

But fortunately whenever the potential for a serious, career-threatening event arises, a million years of genetically preprogrammed survival instincts automatically kick in; all semblance of free will evaporates completely; and I was mechanistically impelled to give the only answer a conniving, corner-cutting, counselor could:

I looked at Vince with a startled gaze and said "Vince — you sly dog — how did *you* know that's exactly what I want to do with my career???"

We now leap forward several years in my story. In spite of my deficiencies in the area of assessment, I landed a job at the University of Houston. There I was — a mere fingerling — swimming in a pool with some *really big suckers*. And they wanted me to summarize my first three years there and tell the story of the rest of my career. Well, what could I say? Something like? : "In the first year I swam after two worms; one got published, the other one got me sick. Remember, in the second year, our stream got polluted, so nobody got any work done. And my third year was a complete wipe-out because I had that run-in with a red-eyed wiggler" (by the way, for those who may not know, that's a fishing lure).

No! I couldn't say that to a departmental review committee, so I told a story about improving methodology by conducting research on research methods. I honestly don't remember if I noticed the slight similarity to the path Vince had urged. Shortly thereafter, Paul Secord taught me the *first principle of ethogeny*, which is "For scientific purposes treat subjects as if they were human beings." And suddenly I was swimming with the current. By tenure review, my story spoke of person-centered methodologies; designs capable of appreciating those uniquely human characteristics like volition, free will, meaningfulness, self-determination, and so forth.

So now I intend to research the psychology of personal freedom. Well, Vince is looking positively prophetic right now. I only wish he could be here to share the moment. [Vince died suddenly a few years ago.]

Many of you realize that I'm going after thorny issues that have plagued students of human nature for several millenia. Do I *really* think I am going to offer something important to that conversation? Frankly, no! For those of you inclined toward a friendly wager, I am currently offering 20 to 1 odds *against* my making a breakthrough. *But isn't that a bet one would love to lose!*

The chairwoman asked me where I'm going. And like Bateson I answer, "You know, that reminds me of a story. . . About a dozen years ago, a good friend dangled a fat, juicy worm in front of a frisky, young sucker, and urged him to swim with it as far as he could. Vince asked me to be a part of a story. And, frankly, it's still the nicest story anyone has ever invited me to take part in."

Well, that's the speech I gave, and that's my best guess as to where my professional story came from — and, more importantly, where it seems to be going.

Giving talks at conventions are adventures that I generally do not enjoy — but my *Quo Vadis* talk was a delight! A number of people in the audience came up to me afterward to tell me their stories of Vince — " I was a grad student at Texas when Vince was director of the counseling center there. I don't believe that he actually let me gather data on . . ."; "You know, Vince waived those stupid summer practicum requirements for me the year before you arrived at SIU. Since I was married and had a family, I had to get a real job. But I felt I could never tell anyone about it because the other students would raise hell, and Vince would get into trouble. It wasn't until you mentioned his waiving the assessment

course for you that I realized — I can't get Vince in trouble" ;
"Remember those poker games Vince used to hold? One night he
was a big winner — and I was the last one out the door — and he
just handed me his winnings. I don't know if he knew it but I was
broke. . . ." [Honesty demands that I question the veracity of that
last report — Vince was *the worst* poker player I ever encountered.
While his generosity goes without question, I simply can't imagine
him winning!]

Now Vince was only human. So I would imagine that
there were some people in the audience who could have told some
true stories where Vince was the villian. But they didn't come
forward to insure that a "fair" or "balanced" or "objective" or
"completely accurate" story of Vince emerged. And I'm glad that
they didn't! At a funeral, you don't tell the family of the deceased
what a jerk the person was. Getting an accurate picture of the life
of the deceased is *not* the point of a funeral. Funerals are for the
living — to help them in their grief process and to urge them to
remember the best in the deceased. After my talk, we were just
trying to remember the best in what Vince gave to us — in the hope
that in the process, we might become better persons ourselves.

Growing older — And growing scareder

> "Are you scared, Daddy?" "No way! It's only thunder."
> — John Gulanick and me

While I still tell our little boys — and myself — that I'm
not scared, the truth of the matter is that I am. Not of thunder — of
course — but of many other things. Life just doesn't seem as safe
to me as it once did. I feel more vulnerable. I think of the future
more than I used to — and that gets me scared. Is it just me? Is it
just "the times"? Is it just the time of my life? John and Greg —
our sons — are now three-and-a-half and two years old. They are
great kids — who seem headed toward good lives. Why then do I
find the prospect of their lives so terrifying? Well, in part, it's
because those cute little fellows *are* so weak, and helpless and
dependent, and unskilled in the ways of the world, and so gullible,
and so trusting, and, and, and. There are lots of things out there
that could be very dangerous for little kids. And for whatever
reason — nature or nurture or both — I am compelled to feel
tremendously responsible. And this imperative extends beyond the
boys. For example, the other day I saw a huge dog chasing a
mother duck and five baby ducks across a golf course. I left my

kids (with friends) and took off like a guided missile after the dog — yelling and snarling and flailing my arms like a wild man. The dog stood its ground for a moment as I got closer. It then began to lope away — snarling and barking over its shoulder as it went. But when it saw me blow right past the ducks and stay hot on its tail, it suddenly dawned upon the dog that "This crazy man really does want a piece of my tail!" The dog quickly demonstrated the evolutionary advantage of four legs relative to two. But the dog was right — I really was desperate to get a piece of him/her. What a stupid thing to want! But the whole episode was not rational — it was visceral. Fortunately, for both me and the dog, Shakespeare isn't always correct — "Beware of what you desire — for you will surely have it" (my paraphrase).

But surely it is less than fair to claim that my kids turned me into a scaredy-cat. Obviously, there is much more to it than just that. Well, I'd hate to ruin a good story by doing something dumb like reviewing some relevant research — so I won't. But I will say that Mary and Ken Gergen have conducted some positively beautiful research on the role of various "plots" in life-narratives (Gergen & Gergen, 1988). But, for the purposes of my story, I'll just "spill the bottom line" of their research now. Here it is — the nature of the plots of life-narratives appear to change, in predictable ways, as people grow older! Earlier in my life I was telling myself a story of my life, and the plot took the form of a comedy-romance narrative. I was the protagonist in an "After a slow start, local boy makes good!" story. It would have made a great movie (Are you listening Hollywood?). But now it's starting to sink in that I already know the ending to the story: I grow old and die! Or perhaps I won't even be afforded the luxury of being allowed to grow old before dying. It's a sad story. The plot of my life-narrative is changing — my life-story is taking on a tragic plot. And, according to the Gergens' findings, it's not just me. Eventually, many people come to see themselves as the central character of a somewhat tragic life-narrative.

Gazing into the crystal ball of one's future is tricky business. It is almost impossible to be thorough and analytical about the unknown. One only catches glimpses of futures which might possibly emerge. But nothing is certain. Consequently, this part of the *Story of George* (and the futuristic thoughts in *A Story of Science*) comes to resemble a stream of consciousness style. Take this next comment as an example. "Every once in a while, I wish Nancy and I had had a dozen kids. But the two we have just about wore me out — so I guess it's for the best."

I can't bid you *adieu* (for now) without first tying down a few (certainly not all) loose ends. These observations take the form of "This is how I see it now — but I could well think differently about it tomorrow." About my childhood and the role my parents played in my formative years: In their views of life, childrearing, and what I would do with my life, they couldn't have been more different from one another. But somehow they made their differences complement each other, rather than clash, with me as the battleground. I see important parts of both of my parents in me — and I am unlike each in other ways. I felt that I was never put in a position where I had to choose between them. Saying I agreed with one (and not the other) on any occasion was fine. The other parent either didn't resent my opinion or hold it against me (or they are both far better actors than I think they are). Being wrong was never a problem — as long as I could say in clear conscience that I was doing my best. They hit me when I was growing up — and I'm really glad they did (of course one of them hit me a lot more than the other did — but don't worry Mom, your secret's safe with me). Sometimes hitting was the only way they could get across the point that I'd simply pushed them too far. And I guarantee I'm a better person because of each and every hit. Well, maybe not for *every* hit.

Another "loose end" that has gotten more of my attention of late involves my tendency to be more than a bit of a workaholic. I have always prided myself in being able to "work anyone else under the table." From early justifications like, "Even though the marks are bad — I can honestly say that I did my very best," I flowed easily into strategies like, "I'm going to work my butt off to prove to those fools at the University of Houston that they made a huge mistake," until now I'm giving myself rather feeble justifications like, "I have to work this hard because, as chairperson, I can't ask the faculty to work harder if I'm not working as hard as I possibly can." Obviously, this "hardworking boy makes good" script has taken over my life, and it is doing with me whatever it will. And perhaps what it is doing is killing me. I have more than my share of "Type A" characteristics. It's stupid beyond belief for someone with those tendencies to do 50 percent of the parenting work for two toddlers, chair a twenty-five person psychology department, and average one book and twelve to fifteen articles per year. I am reminded of Einstein's obsession with finding a unified theory, "I am possessed by a demon!" And the demon is the story we are telling ourselves about what it is we are doing.

And now some of you are nodding and saying to yourselves, "Aha! So that's how these academicians, with golf scores of 125, talk themselves into spending more time on the golf course." But you're wrong! It'll never work — I know myself too well. Golf could never be relaxing for me, because inside this 125-golfer lurks an ex-athlete who dreams of being a 120-golfer — and who is aching to work his butt off to get there. Once again, for me, Mark Twain said it best: "Golf — a beautiful stroll through the country — ruined!"

One final "loose end," and then you'll be done with me — I promise. What to do about God, faith, and death? Well, in the first case, either there is a God or there isn't; in the second, you either have faith or you don't; and in the third case, death is going to come sooner or later. I no longer have the faith I had earlier in life, but I have a feeling a different faith is developing within me now. I'm kind of "between faiths." What should one do in the interim? Rely on your own conscience and do the best you can — I guess. But while in this limbo state, I spend more time in church than most believers. I meditate regularly. I have more discussions with priests and theologians than any other psychologist I know on the Notre Dame campus (I'm either bragging or damning myself with faint praise — you decide) and I'm even now taking a directed readings course in theology. If regaining one's faith involves finding one's way back home — I'm doing everything I can do. I'm working hard at it.

Speaking of finding one's way home, when I was a child we often would visit my grandmother, aunt, uncles, and cousins in upstate New York. My cousin Richie had this great hound dog — Bone Bags! Well, one day old Bonsy got lost — or at least it got dark and he wasn't home yet. We were all somewhat concerned. I was frantic! I wanted to go search for him. My father — who has forgotten more about dogs than any of us will ever know — said, "Green city-kid like you, out in the woods in the dark — no way! Ole Bonsy's been in those woods every day of his life — he'll find a way home. All you can do is leave the back door open, the light on, and every ten or fifteen minutes you go out back and yell as loud as you can 'Bonsy! Come-on home fella!'" So I did. Next morning, Bonsy was there when we woke up — every bit as happy to see us as we were to see him. Now Bonsy was singularly noncommunicative regarding what had gone on the night before, and how he had found his way home. So I guess this story has little insight to share regarding how it is that poor lost souls sometimes come to find their way back home.

Chapter 8

Dare We Develop a Human Science?

It does not "hurt" the moon that I look at it.
("Hurt" meaning "alter the behavior of")

— Albert Einstein

I am reminded of a recurrent theme in certain types of science fiction stories. The master chemist has finally produced a bubbling green slime in his test tubes, the potential of which is great but the properties of which are mysterious. He sits alone in his laboratory, test tube in hand, brooding about what to do with the bubbling green slime. Then it slowly dawns on him that the bubbling green slime is sitting alone in the test tube brooding about what to do with him. This special nightmare of the chemist is the permanent work-a-day world of the psychologist—the bubbling green slime is always wondering what to do about you.

— Don Bannister

You're not going to believe this story — and in fact you shouldn't believe it, because it is pure science fiction. It is a story that couldn't possibly happen — but it is important to remember that the impossible often can illuminate what is commonplace. You guessed it — I'm going to tell another story. But this one is a bit special because you have a role in it. You are telling the story. I'm thrilled that you've made it this far in the book, so I'm going to give you a dynamite part to play. Brace yourself! You are the current holder of the Galileo Galilei, Chair of Astronomy at a prestigious Eastern university. Yes, you are Professor Ivy League! Your career was solid and satisfactory until late one evening as you were taking measurements of a meteor shower, you became the first human to observe what later became known as the League Comet. Discovering a comet would be wonderful in-and-of-itself, but you were doubly blessed because your comet happened to pass within one thousand miles of an unmanned space probe. Since it was "your comet" you were on the ground floor of the group of astronomers and astrophysicists who got immediate access to the data transmitted back to earth by the space probe. But it was your mind — out of those two dozen scientists — that recognized that in those data lay the key to a theory that would (three years later) supercede the Big Bang Theory of the origin of the universe. While you never downplayed the importance of your findings, you maintained the proper level of scientific caution and understatement. Your style caught the eye of an ambitious Provost, who suggested to a donor who wished to remain anonymous, that a Galileo Chair might entice you to the East Coast.

Well, the hubbub about your discoveries has now pretty much subsided, and you are looking forward to a pleasant American Astronomical Association Convention. In fact, you are now walking to the auditorium where you will hear your beloved old dissertation advisor, Professor Big Ten, deliver his Presidential Address to the Association. Suddenly you hear the voice of a classmate, Professor Cal Tech, calling out to you.

"Ivy! Ivy, slow down. I bet you're all excited about hearing The Big One give his Presidential Address. By the way, Ivy, did I ever tell you that you look great in tweed?"

"Oh, Cal! Thank you. It's good to see you. I hope you got a lot done on your sabbatical. Yes, I am looking forward to this talk, but I'm also a bit apprehensive. I called about a week ago to get a sneak preview and our old mentor said the Presidential Address would either be the high or low point of his career — but he couldn't tell which. It's not like him to be uncertain about his work. I hope there isn't any problem. Here's the auditorium. It's mobbed. I hope we can find two seats."

Cal saw two empty seats first. "Here are two. Ivy, what a crowd! Every top astronomer in the world must be here. It's quite a tribute to Professor Ten. Look, he's going to begin."

"This talk is supposed to be the crowning achievement of my career. But I'm afraid that I'm more frightened than a graduate student about to give his or her first public lecture. It should have been a sheer joy to review for you the achievements of my career — to summarize what I've learned over the course of a lifetime devoted to science. But I'm afraid I can't do it. You see, I've been shaken to the very core of my existence these past three weeks. Either I'm on to the greatest astronomical discovery of this or any other century — or I'm crazy as a coot! I'm afraid the odds are long that it's the latter. But please bear with me as I try to say what I have to say as clearly as I can."

Cal grabs your arm and whispers, "Ivy, I don't like this. I hope our friend doesn't do something stupid."

Professor Ten clears his throat and begins nervously, "Well, let me say it and be done with it. Over the past three weeks, I have come to believe that the moon is alive. All along, humans have considered the moon to be an inanimate hunk of rock traveling mindlessly through space. Well, I now believe that that view of the moon is incorrect. You see, the moon has communicated with me telepathically. The moon has told me that it is orbiting in the manner that it does for good reasons, but that it could move in another manner, if it so desired. You see. . ."

Bedlam! Pandemonium breaks out in the auditorium. Some people are yelling, "He's crazy! Get him off the stage!" Others are shaking their heads and saying things like "I can't believe someone would say such things" and "It's simply outrageous that something like this could have happened." Your head is spinning and you seem to be thinking ten different thoughts at once: What is *your mentor* up to?; This must be some sort of a joke; The entire place is in an uproar; Could an entire career of dedication and accomplishment be ruined in one minute?; What a completely preposterous set of claims for anyone — let alone your intellectual idol — to make. Events are moving in a sort of surrealistic slow-motion. You look toward the podium and your heart crumbles completely. Your beloved mentor and friend is leaning heavily against the podium, sobbing softly — a completely broken person. How could everything have gone to pieces so completely, so quickly? You are suddenly gripped with a rage that seems to come from nowhere. You hear yourself shout at the top of your lungs, "Shut up! Everybody, shut up! Be quiet! Shut up! Everybody shut the hell up!!"

Your last command was unnecessary, as it was issued to a completely silent auditorium. The silence suddenly terrifies you because as you look around, all eyes are on you — it's your move — and you haven't the faintest idea of what to do. You look toward the podium and even your mentor is staring at you — startled by your fury.

"Oh Ivy. I'm sorry my friend. This must be so embarrassing for you. I'm terribly sorry that you have to. . ."

"Sorry just won't do it!" you explode. As if by magic, the fury is back and you bark a command to the one person to whom you had never had the temerity to raise your voice. "Those things you said were completely ridiculous. Now, take them back while you still have a chance. You couldn't possibly believe any of the things that you've just said!"

All eyes shift back to the podium. To your utter astonishment, Professor Ten is obviously thinking — weighing what he will say next. What could there possibly be to think about? What is going on here? This has to be absolute insanity — some fool's terrible , twisted idea of a joke!

"I'm sorry, Ivy. I'm afraid I do believe it. The moon is a person — I mean a being — who can freely choose to continue to do what it is doing — or act differently if it so desires. I know that sounds preposterous to you, but I believe it."

Suddenly the rage is back. Almost without thinking you snarl, "Your beliefs don't mean a damn thing! This is science. We don't care what ridiculous beliefs you hold. You must furnish evidence — *hard evidence* — of your beliefs before you as a scientist can make any claim. Where is your evidence? You don't have a shred of evidence to support these outrageous statements. *You* — who made dozens of graduate students and countless thousands of undergraduates *prove* their assertions — how could *you* say anything so stupid?"

Suddenly the old fire flashed again in Professor Ten's eyes. Maybe it was the sight of a former student presuming to lecture him on what science is, or is not — but instantly, you were once again facing that challenging, taunting adversary with whom you've done wonderful battle over the past two decades. "Ivy, might you do me the kindness of considering for a moment that there is not one shred of evidence that is clearly inconsistent with my claim that the moon is simply doing whatever it damn well pleases."

"Wait a minute!" you bark. "Don't give me any of that *Intro to Natural Science* crap about the rules of evidence in science. Professor Ten, so help me, if this is some dumb classroom demonstration technique you're pulling on us, then I'll. . ."

"Relax, my friend." It was clear that the old master was now back in control. "I wouldn't be so stupid as to pull an adolescent stunt like that in a Presidential Address. What do you think? That I'm nuts? Hold it! Don't answer that question just yet. But Ivy, my friend, I'm afraid that I will stick by all of the claims I've made thus far, and ask you as a fellow astronomer to put them to a fair test."

"A fair test? How would one go about testing such a preposterous thesis? I don't even know how to begin to set up a test of that theory." Much to your surprise, a colleague a few rows in front of you raises his hand. Which you quickly acknowledge.

"Excuse me, I'm not sure what is going on here, but I'll say this anyhow. We're in Fort Lauderdale, Florida, right? The Atlantic Ocean lies to the east, right? It's early evening and so, as every astronomer knows, the moon rises in the east in the early evening. Now Professor Ten, since you stated that the moon communicated with you telepathically, I presume that means that you could make statements or requests to the moon." Your mentor nods his assent, and the stranger continues. "OK, here's my proposal. Tell the moon to instead rise in the west tonight, and while I can't speak for everyone here, that would certainly get my attention. I'm not sure I would say that I would be convinced that the moon is a self-determining active agent — but I guarantee that I would be at least nine-tenths of the way toward being convinced."

"No doubt a dazzling demonstration like that would compel everyone to consider seriously the possible validity of my thesis," Professor Ten offered. "But I'm afraid the moon can only alter its own behavior — it cannot perform miracles such as you ask. But I thank you for what I consider to be a friendly suggestion — you are at least trying to put my claim to a fair empirical test."

Suddenly you are intrigued by the stranger's suggestion, and so you inquire further, "Professor Ten, short of a miracle, what would your self-determining moon be willing to show us as evidence that it can influence its own behavior? We'll try to be fair in our requests for evidence that your moon is self-determining, but as scientists we cannot simply accept your claim that the moon is behaving volitionally because we like you, or because we respect your earlier work. Finally, you have us at a disadvantage, Professor Ten, since you are the only one who can communicate with the moon."

"Fair enough, Ivy. We've agreed that we will not ask the moon to perform miracles on the one hand, but if on the other hand I tell you that the moon chooses to continue to behave exactly as it has in the past, you have no reason to believe me. So what intermediate action can we agree upon that will be compelling?'

For the first time in the session, Cal Tech spoke. "Old friend, despite your protests to the contrary, I still believe you are simply leading us upon an intriguing thought experiment. There is simply no way that the moon is an active agent. But since I have always learned quite a lot from your excursions into science fiction fantasy, I'll happily go along on this mind-trip. Here's my proposal: Since we have extraordinarily precise measurements and knowledge of the moon's behavior, if the moon would but alter its orbit by one degree, we would detect it and find the demonstration compelling. And surely asking the moon to alter its trajectory by one degree would not be an overly ambitious request of an agent."

The stranger from several rows ahead, who had spoken earlier, objected, "I'm afraid you've given away too much with that offer. I can think of at least three problems with your proposal. First, no matter how accurate measurements have become in any science, there is still room for error in measurement. I suspect that there will be some controversy regarding whether or not a change of only one degree did or did not occur. Further, a change of that magnitude would not be obvious to the naked eye. I'd like some more dramatic proof — if that isn't asking too much of our active agent moon. Second, imagine that Professor Ten, who is after all a noted astronomer, discovered a force out in space that is traveling toward us. Suppose he calculated that it would engage the moon first, and deflect it from its orbit by one or two degrees. Now with Professor Tech's test of agency, the moon would move a degree or more and suggest (incorrectly) that we were dealing with a lunar agent. Third, as a general rule of thumb, I would want to see some action that reeks of intelligence before I would feel comfortable that the demonstration undeniably was the work of an intelligent agent. For example, if the moon could turn on and off whether or not it reflected the sun's light to us, I would love to see the moon flash on and off a message in morse code — how about 'Moon Person on Board.' That would sure knock my socks off! Or if the moon's agency only enables it to alter its direction of flight, then I'd like to see it dance across the sky in a pattern that writes out in script something like 'Moonperson.'"

Professor Big Ten was obviously tickled with the points being made because he roared with laughter at the thought of the moon writing a letter across the sky to astronomers everywhere. "That would certainly turn quite a few heads in our discipline," he roared, "but I'm afraid that would be asking too much of the moon. But the moon likes the thrust of the stranger's challenge. Set an unusual course for the moon to follow over the next four hours and the moon will follow it. Now, who should we ask to lay out the moon's atypical course? Three people from the audience have spoken up thus far. Since Cal and Ivy are former students of mine, we ought to rule them out to avoid the appearance of collusion. The young man closer to the front who spoke earlier is an astronomer whom I've never met. He might be a good candidate to set the moon's course for the next several hours. Are you game for it, young man?"

With obvious apprehension, the stranger rose and spoke, "The reason that we haven't ever met is because I'm not an astronomer, but rather I'm a psychologist who is interested in the sociology of science. I'm now doing research comparing the topics covered and participants' behaviors at professional meetings for various disciplines. I'm supposed to be an unobtrusive observer at your meeting — not a central player in it. My name is Doctor Santa Barbara. By the way, this session is completely bizarre — not anything like I expected. If you have Presidential Addresses like this every year, I might permanently skip the American Psychological Association convention and come listen to your wild speculations."

As everyone waited for the laughter to subside, you reviewed your feelings. You were a bit embarrassed that this psychologist thought all of your association's Addresses would be as crazy as this one — that certainly wouldn't be good P. R. for the field of astronomy. But you were a bit relieved to hear that the stranger was a psychologist, and not an astronomer. You were more than a bit suspicious when he so quickly came up with three perfectly reasonable objections to Cal Tech's seemingly reasonable suggestion that the moon alter its course by one degree. Your suspicion was based upon the assumption that he was just another astronomer. He should have found all this talk of the moon as an active agent quite unsettling, and the issues of testing for agent self-determination quite novel and perplexing. This Santa Barbara's comments were too lucid and came too quickly to be from someone who was an astronomer and who would have been as shocked at the turn of events as were you. But being a scientific psychologist, you thought, he probably deals with issues of self-determination and active agency daily. That knowledge made his response more believable. Finally, you looked toward the podium and caught your mentor's eye. He managed a weak smile that conveyed enormous relief that your colleagues were taking his preposterous claims seriously for the moment. You saw in the old man a tremendous vulnerability that you had never seen before. You realized his entire career was on the line — bet on what had to be one of the most improbable longshots in the history of science. Frankly, you thought, the hypothesis that the moon is made of green cheese has a much greater likelihood of being true. But because of the personal and intellectual debt you owed to this warm and wonderful human being, you smiled and gave a "thumbs up" signal of encouragement to him — in this, his hour of greatest need.

The stranger began slowly to outline how he would have the moon behave to prove to the audience that it was a self-determining active agent. "You would probably like me to issue the instructions in some kind of space-coordinates — but unfortunately I don't know any. So instead I'll tell you how I want the path of the moon to appear to us here on earth and, Professor Ten, it's then up to you to communicate to the moon what it is to do. OK! Here we go. The moon normally moves across the night sky from east to west. Let's consider that path to be something like a straight line. Now, what I'd like to see the moon do is immediately to move perpendicular to that line. That would make it look as if it made a right-angle turn and is now moving straight up into the night, relative to the path it would normally take. How does that sound? Oh, I almost forgot. I want the moon to triple its speed immediately."

Cal leaned forward and commented rather sardonically, "Shall we then kiss the moon bye-bye forever? Following your commands, our lunar friend is gone forever. At least give me something good to hope for. If the moon continues its current path — my mentor looks foolish. If it makes your right angle veer — our solar system is forever altered. I lose either way."

Santa Barbara took the comment good-naturedly, "Good point! Every potential lover for eons to come would blame *me* for any failed romantic relationship. I don't want that on my head. Moon! One more instruction, please! Maintain the new course for two hours only. Then proceed at your new accelerated speed to the closest possible rendezvous point on your original orbit path. Then proceed at your normal speed and orbit path, until Professor Ten again requests that you change the path of your heavenly flight. Have I undone any possible harm? Are those instructions hopelessly obtuse, Professor Ten?"

The old academician smiled and said, "The instructions are received, understood, and, hopefully, being executed. I guess all that's left to us now is to go outside and see what our lunar friend does. Thank you all for being open-minded enough to entertain these incredibly improbable proposals of mine. I'll see most of you outside, I guess."

You and Cal are swept out of the auditorium by the crowd. Once outside everyone immediately orients themselves, locates the moon, and traces with his or her arm the path the moon will take — if Professor Ten has not been talking nonsense. There is complete agreement as to the moon's normal trajectory at this time of the year. From behind you hear Professor Santa Barbara's voice as he questions Professor Big Ten, "So under normal circumstances the moon would move toward that large building over there? Is that right? OK! So has the moon changed direction and speeded up its movement? What do you think?"

Professor Ten seemed rather surprised to have to break the bad news to the visiting psychologist, "I'm afraid you can't detect the types of changes we're considering with the naked eye until an hour or two has passed. Had we set up the proper instrumentation in advance, we would have known almost instantly whether or not something had changed. But certainly in two hours we will know whether or not the moon's path had been altered. Might I suggest that you, Cal, Ivy, and I go get a cup of coffee and wait for the results of our experiment."

Once comfortably ensconced in a nearby cafe, you were able to follow up with Santa Barbara a few thoughts you had earlier, "I suppose that in your research on human self-determination you have people change their normal behavior patterns in order to demonstrate their ability to self-determine their actions."

"Oddly enough, we don't. I guess we should have been conducting studies of that sort all along, but for years we simply didn't try it. I suspect the reason was because no other science ever offered 'self-determination' as a scientific answer to why their object of investigation behaves as it does. I mean, before today, did astronomers ever offer an answer like 'the moon is following its orbit in order to check out the other side of the earth'? Would any physicist claim that an object fell at a certain speed because it was in a hurry to get to the ground? Or would a chemist claim that sodium combined with chlorine at a low combination temperature because the sodium was anxious to get together with the chlorine? And would any biologist today suggest that the gradual lengthening of the teeth of a species of cats was the result of the cats' desire to have longer teeth? Final causality, agent causality, self-determination, or whatever you want to call such an explanation, seemed to be unscientific in form, and often represented prescientific and amateurish theorizing that was eventually replaced by better, mechanistic, scientific explanations. Remember, a little more than one hundred years ago there were no experimental psychologists. We attempted to free ourselves from the 'dead hand of philosophy,' and to become a science like the other natural sciences. Thus, we developed research methods designed to find the mechanistic, nonagentic causes behind human behavior.

Because that was exactly what the other sciences did. We studied: the effects of various environments upon our behavior; levels of chemicals in our body and how they related to behavior; how early childhood experiences led to later emotional states like depression; how various patterns of family interaction produced stunted relationships; and other mechanistic influences upon humans too numerous to mention. It seems we looked at the forms of explanations in the other sciences and said to ourselves, 'If we can also find explanations of this same type in human action, then we will have performed our function responsibly — we would have developed a properly scientific analysis of human behavior.' That ambition would have been quite appropriate, of course, if human self-determination actually accounted for little or nothing in the genesis of human action. But it is pretty clear to many psychologists now that self-determination is a very important element in human action. Or to answer an ancient philosophical question, 'Yes, reasons can be causes.' But now we are confronted with a huge problem — how does one study such a human capacity scientifically? Obviously, the other sciences are no help to us in this endeavor — for you folks simply assume that your objects of investigation are *not* self-determining. That is, until today that was a standard assumption."

Since Santa Barbara had gotten close to a question that was burning in your heart, you decided to shift gears in the conversation. Addressing your mentor you asked, "Dear friend, why did you do it? Do you really think the moon is communicating with you? Do you really think that when we go outside the moon will have taken a right angle turn and be speeding along on a new path? Did you need to jeopardize your entire career just to test this incredibly improbable thesis? Oh friend, I'm afraid you've exposed yourself to some terribly harsh criticism."

Your mentor was obviously touched by your concern. But even in this, his most desperate hour, the class and humor that was the hallmark of his entire career did not desert him. "Ivy, I wanted to be sure that no one would ever forget my Presidential Address — we've had too many of those boring, nondescript talks of late! And I suppose I could have asked our lunar companion for a sneak preview before I went public with the possibility that the moon could self-determine. But I hope you remember that all my life I have attested that science should be conducted in the public domain. Why should I change my tune now? And think of it — what colossal hubris on my part to say to the moon, 'Perform a trick for my personal edification, and only then will I go public with the message you have entrusted to me.' Do I really think we will find that the moon will have drastically changed its orbit when we return outside? Frankly, it's quite unlikely. But if the moon hasn't changed its orbit, then I guess I have been hearing voices that really aren't there. If that's the case, I think we'd all better face up to that fact — and do whatever we can about it. I'm not terribly frightened, Ivy. With a loving family, and dear friends like you and Cal, I'll be properly taken care of. In fact, things have turned out far better today than I'd expected. When everyone started shouting early on — I thought it was all over. But thanks to you, Ivy, things got settled down again. You never told me that you had background in crowd control. And since the moon has indicated to me that the proposed test of its agency seems fair, who am I to complain? But tell me, friends, what do you think the odds are that the moon has altered its heavenly course?"

You and Cal stared at one another, neither wanting to deliver your pessimistic message, when Santa Barbara voiced his reservations. "I'm sorry, Professor Ten, but I don't think that the moon will have changed its course one iota. But my reasons for believing that the moon cannot change its heavenly path are, I believe, quite different from the reasons that your colleagues might put forward for their pessimism. You see, I have done research on self-determining active agents all my life. Frankly, if we were interested in whether or not a particular person was self-determining, no group of psychologists would assent to the sort of test we put to the moon as being an adequate test of a person's agency. Think about it! Hey fella, make a ninety degree turn and triple your speed, then in two hours return on a diagonal to the spot you would have been at, had you maintained your original course. If you are able to do so, we would be willing to believe that you can self-determine.' The only hard part about that task for a human would be to compute the directional calculations! The real reason that our test of the moon could convince your colleagues is because after long years of study, each is completely convinced that he or she knows exactly what path the moon would have taken had we not intervened to put the test of self-determination to the moon. The power of the experiment, to shake up your colleagues' beliefs regarding the forces that produce the motion of the heavenly bodies, rests on the absolute predictability of the motion of the heavenly bodies under normal circumstances.

But when you make a career of studying active agents — like human beings — you quickly come to realize that prediction of an individual human's behavior by a scientist is almost impossible.

There is simply no way that an auditorium full of psychologists could have come close to agreeing to what a person was going to do under normal circumstances, as we easily did with the predicted path of the moon. Thus, you can see that if a person followed our instructions, like Professor Ten is hoping the moon is now following our instructions, all other psychologists would be unimpressed with that demonstration because (unlike you astronomers) they had no strong belief that the person was going to behave differently had their agency not been challenged experimentally. So you see, while it is much more likely that any person is an agent than is the moon, it is much more difficult to demonstrate this fact experimentally. But the bottom line is that the moon thus far has not acted at all like the other active agents we have studied over the years. Thus, I don't believe the moon is able to self-determine, and so I think its course will be unchanged."

Your curiosity has been aroused by this excursion into experimentation with humans, and you ask, "Well, then, is there no way in which a social scientist can ask a subject to perform a particular pattern of actions that will furnish evidence of his/her ability to self-determine his/her actions? I mean, if you really believe that humans can self-determine their behavior to some degree, then you should have developed some research techniques or methodologies that would demonstrate this ability."

"Well, yes, we do have some techniques that accomplish precisely this task, but they are far more complex in nature than the experimental task that we put to the moon to prove its ability to self-determine its behavior. In short, these methodologies ask humans to embark upon a pattern of actions that we know in advance cannot be produced by any mechanistic cause or set of causes. Now, there is a complex set of methodological arguments necessary to justify my last claim — and I suspect your minds are on other topics — like what the moon is now doing. Thus, I'll spare you that line of reasoning for now."

Cal looked at his mentor sadly. "Well, old friend, it has been about an hour since the moon should have begun its new, self-determined course. If it veered, it will surely be obvious to us by now. I guess it's time to face the music."

You and Cal instinctively drape your arms around your mentor's shoulders and the three of you walk in synchrony toward the door. "Cal, Ivy, I can't tell you how happy I am to have you with me for my Presidential Address. Friendship is a very important part of life."

Santa Barbara picked up the bill and watched the trio head

for the door. How odd, he thought, to have three world-class scientists marching out together, each hoping desperately to see the evidence that will completely undermine the contributions of their long careers. Was this a tribute to scientists' lust for Truth at all costs, or an indication of the power of friendship?

We are spinning our own fates, good or evil, and never to be undone.
Every smallest stroke of virtue or of vice leaves its never so little scar . . .
Nothing we ever do is, in strict scientific literalness, wiped out.
— William James

Well, did you like the story? This was my way of making the transition from psychology conceived of as a natural science to psychology conceived of as a human science. The remainder of this chapter will probe some of the ways in which a human-scientific psychology of the future might develop. But like the previous chapter — *Quo Vadis*? — all a futurist can do is to note present trends or recent innovations and extrapolate them into the future. The hope is that in telling the story of such an imagined future, we can work to make the future that does occur better than the one that would have occurred, had the futurist not spun his or her tale of the future.

Did you notice that I told you a lie at the beginning of the story about the moon and Professor Big Ten? I told you at the outset that the story was impossible — that it couldn't possibly happen. That prediction was incorrect! The story could easily occur — and might yet. But when I wrote the line about the impossibility of it happening, I thought that I would have to have the moon dancing across the evening sky in some bizarre fashion in order to make my points regarding methodology in science, putting theories to a fair empirical test, and important differences in prediction and/or explanation for a science where self-determination, will, agency, personal causation, volition, and so forth is central (like psychology), as opposed to a natural science (like astronomy). In the telling of the story, it became clear that the points I wanted to make could be done with fiction alone. It was unnecessary to resort to science fiction to make them. In fact, much of what this book offers is an elaboration of how important storytelling has become in science (stories are often referred to as "thought experiments") and how absolutely vital stories will be for the science and practice of a psychology of the future.

Social scientists who pursue research activities whenever possible study large samples of subjects for two admirable scientific reasons: 1) to be methodologically rigorous and objective; and 2) to be consonant with science's larger objective of establishing general principles or laws. In some domains of the social sciences the practical goals of the discipline are consonant with the above principles and thus, I would argue, methodologies considering large groups of subjects are quite appropriate. Election polling is one such example.

But there is a troubling relationship between any individual subject and the behavior of the group. Long ago William James called this problem *the psychologist's fallacy*. The fallacy occurs whenever the empirical properties of data are uncritically assumed to reflect psychological properties of the individual persons, observations of whom generated the analysis of those data. Researchers in psychology make that fallacious assumption almost universally. Consider an instance where the fallacy is present — but for the purposes of the experimenters, it is not at all troublesome. Imagine an election where 90 percent of the voters have a slight preference for candidate A and 10 pecent a slight preference for candidate B. The conclusion is that candidate A is *overwhelmingly* preferred. But according to our example no individual has more than a slight preference for candidate A. Conversely, if 51 percent adamantly endorse candidate A while 49 percent are equally committed to candidate B, one would conclude that voters have a *slight preference* for candidate A. In reality, there isn't a *slight* preference in the house. But surely you are thinking "So what!" In both cases, the outcome of the election (a group-level phenomenon) is accurately predicted. I agree. The psychologist's fallacy is present, but it poses no problem for the purposes of that particular study.

But now let's apply the same methodology to the question posed in the fictitious story posed earlier in this chapter. Can planets — like the earth's moon — self-determine their orbits? Using the most honored group-research methodologies, one might select twenty planets in our solar system and issue the instructions Professor Santa Barbara gave to the earth's moon to all twenty planets. Imagine that only one planet — the earth's moon — adhered to these instructions and the other nineteen continued along their eternal orbits. Since exactly one out of twenty deviant findings is expected to occur by chance, if the null hypothesis (that planets can self-determine) were true, we would claim with great confidence that these data do not suggest planets' abilities to self-determine. But we've already agreed (I hope) that if the moon behaved in the manner described, we would be quite convinced. Further, imagine (although I wager none of us really believe this) that all planets are active agents who are able to self-determine their heavenly flight. Might not nineteen out of twenty think something like the following: "*I could easily perform that little dipsey-doodle in the sky that these puny humans request. But what galls me is the collossal hubris of these people. The nerve of them to suggest that I should perform a trick for their edification. I am going to continue in my present orbit, and if they draw the wrong conclusion regarding my nature, that's their problem. Besides, they never even asked me to sign an informed consent document!*" The immediate point to be made is that *the psychologist's fallacy* renders our data-based conclusions completely incorrect in this hypothetical example. But now compare the planets' decision *not* to alter their orbits with my claim that the reason I am now able to exercise regularly is due in large part to my concerns about a possible heart attack. While in all likelihood it is not true that planets are active agents, in all likelihood it is true that I am. Applied psychologists have always presumed agency in human beings — scientific psychology has precluded the possibility of finding agent self-determination in their empirical investigations.

Can you even imagine how one would design a scientific study (that would be acceptable for publication in a journal) where the conclusion would be that people acted in a certain way "because they felt like it," or "because it seemed like the right thing to do," or "because they wanted to see what would happen if they acted in that way," and so forth. Well, the good news is that such designs are just now emerging. As promised in the Preface to this book, Chapter 12 will sketch a scientifically appropriate model for psychology that treats agent self-determination as the central explanatory construct in appreciating human behavior. The model also shows how the traditional material and efficient causes studied by psychologists form a backdrop against which agent deliberation occurs, and thus are real, important influences in the action we choose to take. But from this perspective a "reason" can be a "cause," and often is.

How is this agent self-determination achieved? The initial evidence suggests that meaningfulness is an important characteristic. Or stated somewhat differently, a "good reason" can be a "strong cause." And it is the presumption of this book that applied psychologists — like clinicians — have been correct all along in that people connect the events, facts, circumstances, and situations of their lives through narrative accounts. *They tell themselves stories about what is going on in their lives.* In so doing life becomes far more than "just one damn thing after another."

So there you have *A Story of Science* up to the present. As with any story, lots was left out. But like evolutionary phylogeny, much of science, while real, is simply irrelevant to the points that I wanted to make. It is also a hopeful story — I think bright days lie ahead for a scientific study of agent self-determination, and psychologists will lead the way. I also believe that, in time, this fruitful research program will expand and enrich our notion of scientific rationality itself. I hope Ernan McMullin will not yell at me for saying this, but I believe that philosophy of science should never be prescriptive or proscriptive — it should not tell scientists what they should or should not do in science. Rather, philosophers of science should reflect upon successful scientific programs and extract whatever lessons they can from these episodes. Philosophy of science *is* what good science *does*. What will eventually prove successful in science can never be known in advance either by philosophers of science or by scientists. Remember, Ernan, that the clouds never parted so that God could tell us how to do good science. We've all got to muddle through our careers, figuring out what is going on, by whatever lights are given to us. So, if I've roused your anger in my construal of the relationship between science and philosophy of science, please remember the words of one of my favorite songs: "Be not too hard, for life is short, and nothing is given to man."

Chapter 8 1/2

Do You Know the Difference between Wisdom and Knowledge?

It was a species which often considered itself to be,
basically, a race of divinely inspired toolmakers; any
intelligent entity from Arcturus would instantly have
perceived them to be, basically, a race of impassioned
after-dinner speechmakers.

— Walter M. Miller, Jr.

In the Preface of this book the author brought you this far,
and then rather cryptically promised to analyze the two stories in the
remaining chapters. Did you really think that I would shift gears
stylistically and provide a traditional, scholarly analysis of the
characteristics of narrative or storytelling approaches to
understanding? Be serious! I'm having too much fun writing
stories, and spinning stories within stories, and embedding images
within stories about storytelling. I just don't have the heart to
discipline myself to write an analysis of narratives in "scholarese."
Besides, Mair (1977), Sarbin (1985), and Polkinghorne (1988)
have already conducted such scholarly analyses of narratives —
and done it far better than I possibly could. If you now have a
hankering for serious, solid, sober, scholarly analysis on this topic,
please read the three references above.
What I'd like to do is to play with a few ideas about
storytelling in the hope that you will come to see the narrative root
metaphor for human knowledge in a somewhat different (and I
hope more plausible and practical) light. Simultaneously, I will
also play with some other topics (such as psychotherapy, teaching,
research in psychology, friendship, religion, commonsense
knowledge, and so forth) with which you have some familiarity,
and elaborate these topics from the storytelling perspective.
Remember, Sarbin's (1985) remarkable claim that (virtually all of)
"psychology is narrative" suggests that disparate, commonplace
human activities should then be understandable from this
storytelling perspective. You know, it's funny, but the more I
think about it, the more I agree with Sarbin's claim. I'll try to flesh
out the storytelling thesis as stridently as I am able. And since
you've made it this far in this story of storytelling, I assume you

haven't found the writing style completely objectionable. So I'll try to make my points within the context of stories that are as intrinsically interesting as possible — arguments with real people, discussions with imaginary people, classroom conversations, jury trials, psychotherapy sessions, and the like. I'll do my best to make the points within the context of interesting stories. I hope you like them.

The last section of this book is built around themes in storytelling (e.g., the role of accuracy versus utility in telling stories; the importance of the storyteller's perspective; the role of hope in stories; the role of wisdom as opposed to knowledge in human lives; the question of a science of storytelling; and others) and some important human activities (e.g., work, religion, psychotherapy, psychological research, friendship, etc.).

Here is a brief preview of what is to come:

Chapter 9: We consider some longstanding, troublesome problems such as: whether human nature is best understood scientifically or artistically; the mind-body problem; and the scientist-practitioner schism within psychology. The medium for examining these issues is a dialogue with an imaginary therapist — Doc. The topic of our conversation involves what might be the best understanding of how it is that psychotherapy succeeds — when it does work.

Chapter 10: Doc presents a transcript of one of the therapy sessions she conducted with a client. Doc explicitly shows a model of doing therapy that is simultaneously both good science and good practice. She also sketches a model of humans that integrates agency and mechanistic determination within a framework of humans as self-construing active agents. That Doc is one hell of a woman! But, unfortunately, just when the issues seem to move toward happy resolutions, the session delves into deeper problems: the free will - determinism controversy and the relationship of science to religion. Sigh! That's the problem with good therapy sessions, they go wherever they will — you just can't control them.

Chapter 11: Stories are told for many different reasons. The purpose behind the telling of any story is a critical determinant in a variety of issues, such as: Is it more important that this story be factually accurate, engrossing, or potentially useful for the storyteller? Oh, I almost forgot that you might be interested in the outcome of the lawsuit discussed in this chapter. While the jury is still out, the odds are 3 to 1 that I'll win an acquittal.

Chapter 12: Students in an honors social science class force me to get explicit about the nature of human beings who are self-determining active agents. We also struggle to integrate and refine some of the themes (such as free will versus determinism, science and religion, the purpose of life, etc.) considered earlier in the book.

Chapter 13: Do you know the difference between knowledge and wisdom? I can think of several people who are knowledgeable but unwise, and a few who are wise but lack knowledge in many important domains. All such individuals will remain nameless. Another psychologist, who is also a dear friend, Howard Sandler, and I discuss "wisdom" to shed whatever light on this important skill-for-living that we are capable of generating. Thank you for your help, Howard. Left to my own devices, I couldn't have lit a 40-watt bulb in the wisdom domain.

Chapter 14: This chapter ties up some loose ends and explicitly states the themes that run through the book. We turn (metaphorically) toward the future to imagine the characteristics of an integrated science and practice of psychology of the future. This model is grounded in the view of humans as self-constructing and storytelling active agents.

Throughout the remainder of this book, one will sense a palpable tension between the roles of knowledge and wisdom in one's life. For extended scholarly treatments of this topic, one might consider Bellah *et al.'s* (1985) *Habits of the Heart*; Schwartz's (1986) *The Battle for Human Nature*, and MacIntyre's (1981) *After Virtue*. Science can tell us a good deal about *how* things function—this is (roughly) the domain of knowledge. Scientific psychology can tell us a good deal about how it is that people actually do function. But, for human beings, the question of *how people ought to live their lives* is also very important—this is (roughly) the domain of wisdom. Since science can tell us little (or nothing) about how we *ought* to live our lives, we begin to glimpse some of the roots of the scientist-practitioner problem in psychology, since psychotherapy frequently centers around questions of *how one ought to lead his or her life*. In *A Story of George* my reflections on "why I think, act, and feel the way I do" are of interest to me-as-a-scientist. But of even greater importance to me-as-a-person are questions about: what would make my life worth living; what values should permeate my relationships with others; what is the place of the spiritual in my life; and what are my proper responsibilities to my family, friends, profession, country, and the human race? For glimmerings of answers to such questions, one would be ill-advised to query science! Instead, *wisdom* should be sought from the humanities, the arts, and enduring cultural institutions such as the family, religion, and the schools, for knowledge is insufficient to give purpose to one's life. Purpose and meaning exist when one sees himself or herself as an actor in some larger story—be it a cultural tale, a religious narrative, a family saga, a political movement, and so forth. Finally, pity the poor psychotherapist who must understand and promote facilitative change in human lives. Such individuals must be more than scientists—for the wisdom considerations of how one ought to lead one's life permeate therapy. But therapists must also have command of the technologies for helping people to change—for psychology has extensive knowledge of how such programs might best be effected. My hat is off to any soul brave enough to accept a job description that requires competence in the domains of both knowledge and wisdom. A part of wisdom is being able to recognize and decline challenges that are too great for one's competence. My decision to be a scientific psychologist looks better and better to me with every passing day.

> Two roads diverged in a wood, and I—
> I took the one less traveled by,
> And that has made all the difference.
> —Robert Frost,
> *The Road Not Taken*

Chapter 9

Stories Gone Mad!

The first step towards madness is to think oneself wise.

— Fernando de Rojas

Before reflecting upon the characteristics of all forms of storytelling (and analyzing these characteristics as they appeared in *A Story of George* and *A Story of Science*), I need to remind you of a recent remarkable, technological creation — modern psychotherapy. Recall that children create "imaginary playmates" with whom they talk from time to time. Within limits, it is a normal, healthy activity for a child to undertake. Similarly, within limits, it is a normal, healthy activity for a psychologist to create and converse with an "imaginary psychotherapist." My imaginary psychotherapist is named Doc. I'll let you in on a conversation she and I had recently that dealt with the question "What makes psychotherapy work?" It does work, you know! Here's the conversation:

"Hey, George! How's it going?"

"Not bad, Doc. But I do have a pretty bad case of intellectual constipation. I know what I want to say in this *Tale of Two Stories* book, but the words aren't coming out right. I'm not doing a good job of getting from 'here' to 'there.'"

"Too bad. But be thankful — at least you've got something you want to get out, and you do know where you want to wind up. Perhaps if you tell me where you want to end up, I might be able to help you work backward to where you are now."

"OK! As you know, in your job as a psychotherapist you listen to your clients' stories about their lives, problems, ambitions, and current difficulties. You need to know each client's story in order to get the necessary background to be able to help them to see their life, goals, problems, and so forth in a different, more healthy light. That's the heart of psychotherapy — isn't it?"

"Well, 'yes' and 'no,' George. I mean, psychotherapists could 'see' what they are doing in quite different ways. But I agree with you that clients come to therapy because their lives have gotten out of control in some way. The therapist's task is to help them to reestablish control in some way—and then to get out of the client's life. I'm furious about charlatans who insinuate themselves into their clients' lives and hook them on being dependent on their therapist."

"Whoa, Doc! Do I detect some anger beneath your normally mellow, facilitative veneer?"

"Shove it! I'm pissed all right. But I'm more pissed at you than I am at the run-of-the-mill hack therapist. I was reading over your shoulder as you wrote that *Story of George*, and while I really liked some of it, some of it scared me to death. I mean, I can handle self-destructive behavior in my clients with an appropriate degree of professional detachment that enables me to intervene effectively. But when I think of your self-destructive lifestyle, I get terrified. I mean, if you spring a leak somewhere in your cardiac tubing and buy the farm — *it's lights out for me too!*"

"I'm sorry, Doc. I didn't think that I'd be scaring you, too. . ."

"Listen! I've been telling you for years that you've been burning the candle at both ends for too long — you gotta change or we're history!"

"I've been trying to change my ways — but I just can't seem to ease off the accelerator. Maybe things will be different next year when I'm on sabbatical."

"George, I wish I could believe that stepping down as department chair would change things — but you know as well as I that the circumstances of your life are only a small part of the problem. The core of the problem is that your story has gone mad. Your story, about a hard-working boy from Bayonne who works his butt off and actually makes a contribution, has almost completely taken you over. The story is out of control — and you are simply the vehicle that is careening about — carrying that story to a perhaps-tragic ending."

"Right, Doc! Let me get out my DSM III and look that one up. Let me see. Hmmm — nothing in the index under 'Story Nut.' Maybe I should try 'bibliopath'. . ."

"Go ahead, joke about it. But you're going to be the same old workaholic when the laughter stops. At your funeral, no one is going to feel much like remembering your best one-liners. **When are you going to realize that doing less work is serious business?"**

"I'm, sorry, Doc. But it's so frustrating to think about these things. I mean, you take risks in life — spiritually, professionally, intellectually, financially, in love, in having children, in everything. And for awhile the uncertainty of these risky wagers is really heady stuff. You find yourself wheeling and dealing with life — and it's exciting. And then slowly but surely it begins to wear you down. The excitement of it all is replaced by a kind of dread that seeps into your bones, and simply tires you out. And when you feel weak and sober from this weight, you look for some ultimate ground on which to stand. Some people find it in God! Some people find it in the size of their bank account! Some people find it in family! I guess some people never find any solid ground at all! For me it's been a little of all of these mixed with a basic humanistic impulse guided by 'Do unto others as you would have them do unto you.'

"But all of this is too easy, and represents only vague generalities. Somehow I have come to believe that one must be suffering in some way for life to be meaningful. Unless there is a supreme effort, or uncommon dedication, then one might have led a bland (and therefore meaningless) existence. Think of Tom Dooley and Mother Theresa serving the most unfortunate! Consider Dag Hammarskjold's commitment to public service! Think of Albert Einstein's love of the truth! What of Ludwig Beethoven's passion for beauty in music? And what special demon drove William Shakespeare to paint the wonder of the human condition in the oils of prose more richly than any other human? And how were Mahatma Ghandi and Martin Luther King, Jr., able to bend human nature to make nonviolent resistance part of their lifestyle? Are we not members of the same species as these giants? How can we possibly settle for the puny lives we choose to live?"

"Of course, George, you must remember that Ghandi's relationship with his son was always troublesome, and caused the Mahatma great pain. And you know that Hammarskjold was never able to develop a satisfying relationship with his spouse. Suppose the devil offered you a deal — be psychology's Newton but have a poor relationship with your wife or your sons. Would you take that deal? That throws a different light on the issue — doesn't it? You have to keep the whole picture in mind. Greater success is, at first blush, always to be desired. But is it still desirable when we

count the costs of success? Remember Shakespeare's observation in one of his darker moments, 'Beware of what you desire — for you will surely have it.' But I guess I should ask a more basic question first. George, do you have the seeds of greatness in you? Are you psychology's Newton — who is simply failing to achieve his destiny because of laziness?"

"No, Doc, of course not. I couldn't have that destiny because of a lack of 'G' — you know, raw intelligence, candlepower, brains, whatever. I think I have a quick, creative mind — and a great grasp of basic common sense. Those aren't unimportant skills — and I have the gall to think I have used them quite well in my career. But I just don't have the intellectual power of others I know — like Scott Maxwell, Sandra Scarr, Ernan McMullin, Tom Cook, Valerie Tarico, and others. It's not false modesty on my part, they're just smarter than I am — pure and simple. So what! That's just the way it is. Oh — this is funny — in college, when I announced that I was switching from being a math major to a psych major, everyone in my family tried to be supportive of my decision — but one could easily see BIG MISTAKE written all over their reactions. Well, to everyone's surprise, my old Irish grandmother, Margaret Jordan, announced in her thick Irish brogue, 'Well now, one could make quite a contribution, if one just made sure that psychologists had a firm grasp of the obvious. You might see if you could get that job.'

"In many ways, that's what my career has been all about. Everything I've found about humans in my research has been perfectly obvious. Being obvious is good, on the one hand, because I never really seriously doubt the basic validity of my findings. But, on the other hand, since the findings are so transparently self-evident, I have a *So what!* reaction. Am I just wasting my life demonstrating the obvious? You know, Doc, I think I'm getting clearer on what is the crux of my problem. You know how economists get stopped short when they're asked, 'If you're so smart (about economics), how come you ain't rich?' Well, a parallel critique of psychology might be, 'If you're so smart (about life, or human behavior), how come you're so screwed up?'"

"You mean, if we know so much about human motivation — why are we so often undermotivated ourselves; or pathology, why are we so crazy ourselves; or child rearing, why are our kids such problems; and so forth?"

"Yep Doc, that's it! As a group, why are we so unwise? Wisdom — that's the missing ingredient here. Think about it. How is research in psychology — or the research training psychology graduate students get — going to make them wiser persons?"

"Eureka! I've been sitting here thinking just that for years — and all you ever do is read those dreadful books on research methodology and philosophy of science. George, honestly, sometimes I think that the only thing you use your right brain for is a hat-rack! Scott Maxwell says read a book on *Quasi-experimentation* and you spend a week boring me with that stuff. Ernan McMullin mentions that *Philosophy and the Mirror of Nature* is good, and you drop everything to plow through it. But let Rosemary Phelps suggest *The Women of Brewster Place*, and just because it's a novel, you won't let yourself read it. The only time you'll even consider reading *real* literature is when you are on vacation. You simply don't take the time and effort to plunge into the human experience in any meaningful way.

"I agree with you that research and research training don't make psychologists any wiser as people — but I believe that clinical training can make one a wiser person. Let me be a bit more precise in saying that — doing psychotherapy can make you a wiser person. But you have to have a good attitude in doing therapy. You have to want to learn from the client — to be touched by the story that the client lays out for you. If a therapist approaches people with an openness toward being changed by them, therapy can be a deepening, enriching experience. The therapist sometimes emerges from therapy as a richer, fuller, or — using your terms — a *wiser* person."

"Well now, Doc, you've got to help me out on this a bit, so that I'm sure I've got it straight. A client comes to you as a therapist, and the client tells you his or her story—which frequently is a crazy story. By that I suspect that you mean that the story now is maladaptive in some way. For example, while my 'I can work anyone under the table' theme was extremely useful to me throughout my life, that part of my story is now somewhat destructive. Now I presume this change came about either because I have exaggerated the theme to inappropriate dimensions of late, or because the circumstances of my life changed so that what was once an appropriate theme, now represents a potentially dangerous stance for me to take. Well, that's an interesting thesis, but biologically-oriented clinicians won't like that approach a bit, and I would think you'd be hard pressed to explain how, for example, a depressed person who takes an antidepressant drug comes to feel better. Surely you are not going to claim that Elavil acts to rewrite a mad story line."

"No, I wouldn't claim that, of course. Remember, George, an antidepressant doesn't cure the depression — it simply treats the symptoms. But you see, the mind-body problem is no problem at all for me. After all *I don't have to believe* everything *you* read in those philosophy books. I see 'mind' influence 'body' every day. And just as often I see clients' bodies influencing their thinking. There's no great problem or mystery here for me. But then again, I don't have to explain the precise relationship between mind and body in prose to the professional audience. As Heideigger said, 'We can know more than we can tell, and we can tell nothing without relying upon our awareness of things we may not be able to tell.' For me, the mind-body problem is no problem at all. I understand how mind and body work — I just can't tell you exactly the mechanisms whereby they work together. But returning to the use of antidepressants, I'd just say that troubled stories produce physical effects — the neurochemistry of the body becomes altered. Correct the maladaptive aspects of the story, and the body is free to correct the chemical imbalances. That is, the body becomes able to heal itself. Or consider a client who must make profound alterations in his or her life-story. If by chemical intervention we are able to achieve a more facilitative seasoning of the cerebrospinal soup, this could make our efforts at rescripting or rebiographing much easier and more likely to achieve success. But this is just a simple application of Lazarus' (1976, 1985) principle that multimodal influences are more likely to achieve success than single-mode interventions."

"Oh Doc, I love it when you talk scholarly to me! But didn't I hear you subtly 'up the ante' in this conversation when you moved from language about 'telling life-stories slightly differently' to 'efforts at rescripting and rebiographing'? It sounds like we're now into some heavy-duty, major-overhaul-of-personality treatment."

"Well, yes and no. Some people have basically healthy stories with some minor wrinkles that might be ironed out a bit. If I thought it wouldn't go to your head, I might put *your story* in that group, George. You know, mildly neurotic, minor life-adjustment problems."

"Call me anything but late for supper! By the way, while you're under the hood, would you check the oil and battery also?"

"But some people have very destructive, self-defeating life stories. And after years of being a careful observer of the human condition, a clinician begins to see patterns emerging from this welter of life stories. Some types of stories will sooner or later get a person into serious trouble. One of the few good books you've read of late, George, is *Scripts People Live* by Claude Steiner. It speaks of habitual patterns of relationships that some people develop and then impose upon many — sometimes all — of their relationships. It's as if these people create a story about the pattern that a relationship should take, and then they recreate that pattern in as many of their relationships as possible. George, I was delighted to see you try to get explicit in Chapter 13 (Pumping Karma) about the type of relationship you strive to establish with people you like and trust. It was wonderful of Howard Sandler to help you put that on paper — he's a darling of a man. Of course, the relationship that does occur between you and someone else is a mixing of the relationship you pull for, with the type of relationship the other person desires. Some stories complement each other — some stories clash. Think about *A Story of George*. Some people will be attracted to it — others will be put off and suspicious of it. Having different people react in diametrically opposite directions to the exact same story is only natural."

"Doc, I just remembered that Jane Loevinger (1987) claimed that the fact of Freud's success in working with patients with hysterical paralysis might not have been due to his theory of psychodynamics. She thought that since these clients could move their paralyzed limbs when under hypnosis, that the medical profession considered them malingerers. And so, instead of allowing these patients to tell their story, *they* were accused of bad faith and resistance. Freud came along and urged them to tell their stories. Loevinger suggested that it might be this storytelling — and the inevitable story revisions — that represented the curative mechanism in Freud's success. Freud's psychodynamics represented a set of conceptual glasses through which he viewed the development of the client's problems, but it is quite possible that his psychodynamic theories were really irrelevant to the cure. Freud's theoretical views led him to allow the person to tell his or her story — which began the client's own work of rebiographing — which could have been the real curative element. Of course, Carl Rogers (1961) later developed a theoretical model which speculated that a person first tells his or her story, and then looks into his or her own being (specifically, the client gets in touch with his or her *organismic valuing process*) and finally becomes able to reorient his or her own life. In this client-centered approach, the therapist merely provides a facilitative relationship (marked by the therapist's nonpossessive warmth, accurate empathy, and genuineness) in which a client can redirect his or her own life. Such an approach sees the client doing the script rewriting with the therapist merely providing a safe environment for this rebiographing to occur. From this perspective, Freud and Rogers seem to be helpful to clients more in the way that we understand ministers, guidance counselors, best friends, paraprofessionals, and others to be of help to people looking to make changes in their lives."

"Well, George, I think I agree with **95 percent of** what you say. A part of the work of any good psychotherapist has to do with developing a good working relationship (sometimes called a therapeutic alliance). This part is what other helpers also offer, and what aids their helpees in making helpful life changes. I'll go one step further on this point. In establishing this relationship the skills, attitudes, and perspectives of the sensitive artist, the liberally educated humanist, and the natively caring down-to-earth human being are implicated at least as much as *any possible professional training* one might receive in this domain. Bright, caring, sensitive people (regardless of professional training) make good helpers in this domain of the relationship building, maintenance, and utilization aspect of therapy. The helper acts more as an artist (right brain orientation) in this aspect of the change process.

"But being a professional psychotherapist also involves a sciencelike component, which often requires technical training, and always requires serious study of how humans act, react, develop, succeed, think, feel, and most important, how humans change. Now a psychotherapist thinks and acts like a scientist in this domain because he or she analyzes life situations, theorizes about the critical factors implicated, hypothesizes how changes in the person's life-story, life circumstances, or whatever will achieve results, and initiates changes based upon this quasi-theoretical analysis."

"Quasi-theoretical analysis? Doc, I always knew you were a 'closet scientist.' Correct me if I'm wrong, but this scientistlike part of the clinician might even use successful theories more often in the future, abandon unsuccessful theories, modify partially helpful theories, and so forth. In so doing, the clinician would be acting like a good empiricist.

"So let me make a proposal, Doc, and you tell me if you like it. Excellent psychotherapy is a *craft* that is largely the job of rewriting maladaptive life-stories. A craftsman (like a maker of beautiful pottery) needs not only the sensitivity of the artist to produce the beauty and appeal of the product but also the knowledge and skill of the scientist/technician to mold and produce a durable, workable product. So the excellent psychotherapist possesses the sensitivities, insight, and perspective of the humanist/artist, wed to the theoretical knowledge and technical skills of the scientist. Is that close to being correct?"

"Close enough! Remember, I say scientistlike part in order to reemphasize that while the clinician utilizes knowledge from scientific theoretical perspectives, and results of studies on humans, one does not necessarily become a better clinician either by being trained to be a scientist or by doing research on humans. While the products of science might make us all better clinicians, the process of science itself does not make one a better clinician. Finally, I must add that artists are both born and developed. So now let's consider the artistic component of the excellent therapist. Basic personal and interpersonal skills are essential. But these basic attributes can be honed,

refined, and polished greatly in either of two quite
different ways. The first obvious way is through
professional training — like basic interpersonal skills
courses, professional supervision and feedback,
observing skilled therapists at work, reading case
analyses by gifted therapists, and reading conceptual
analyses of human nature and change processes.
Actually doing therapy is also essential. Now someone
could have all of those experiences and remain
none-the-wiser for the experiences. It is necessary for
the person to possess an attitude of openness, a
willingness to experience new perspectives, a desire to
become a more sensitive, cultured, literate, and wise
person because of the experiences. If people enter any
of the above training experiences believing they know it
all, have the answers already, or possess all that it
takes to be an effective helper — they will emerge as
the same ineffective, egotistical bores they were when
they began the experience. We all know plenty of
'helpers' who fit that description. A therapist
'in-dwells' in the life (or story) of the client. Out of
this in-dwelling in many such lives comes insight and
wisdom as to how to help the client to right himself or
herself. But the therapist in his or her in-dwelling must
be willing to be changed through the process. One
must be open to being touched by another's life to
become wiser for the experience. If you think you have
already 'got all the answers,' all you'll ever be able to
hear is yourself — giving those same old answers.

"But I mentioned that there is a second way in
which a person can achieve the artistic wisdom
necessary to become an excellent therapist. Such
sensitivities might be nurtured through a good liberal
arts education. One can in-dwell in a novel, or a
biography, or an autobiography in exactly the same way
that a therapist in-dwells in a client's life-story. And if
the reader is open to being changed by experiencing the
text, he or she can grow in wisdom in that way. The
same might said of visiting a different culture through
sociology or anthropology; a different spiritual realm
through theology; a different age through history; and
so forth. I can honestly say that my view of human
behavior was profoundly altered by two books by

economists: Thomas Schelling's *Micromotives and Macrobehavior;* and E. F. Schumacher's *Small is Beautiful*. Each of those books has done more to make me a better psychologist than about 95 percent of the books on psychology that I've read."

So, many people have the wisdom necessary to meet the artistic needs of the complete therapist package. In Chapter 10, Doc and I will again discuss the role of the scientist/technician aspect of psychologists' training in forming the complete therapist. We'll also explain exactly how clinicians use scientific theories and evidence to mold and inform their work with clients. In effect, we try to reintegrate the "scientist" and "practitioner" parts of psychologists in a manner that not only honors human nature in all its intricacy and subtlety but also leads to more precise and effective means of helping people therapeutically. I guess you'll be the judge of exactly how well we achieve that lofty ambition.

Chapter 10

Reflections on Life, Science, and the Role of Therapy in the Pursuit of Happiness

Everything should be made as simple as possible, but not simpler.

— Albert Einstein

"It's a sad tale but true, Doc. The time demands upon me grew slowly at first: work on another committee; supervise another thesis; develop a new course; take part in a faculty reading group; and so forth. Then the cataclysmic events began to occur: taking the director of graduate studies job; the birth of my son John; chairing the psychology department; and the arrival of John's brother Greg. Even as we talk, my mind wanders back to a simpler, less frantic time — to those pastoral days when I was an assistant professor. Oh, I was busy back then — and pressured too. What assistant professor isn't? But it is almost literally true that apart from meeting two classes each week and getting some sleep, my time was my own. Lots to do — but 168 hours each and every week in which to do it.

"Life was good back then. I was bursting with energy, enthusiasm, and bright ideas. Life is good now, too. The pleasures of family and career are difficult to describe, but real nonetheless. And while I've got no complaints overall, I do have a few regrets about my life as I now live it. For example, I finally forced myself to step onto a bathroom scale several months ago. I knew the news would be bad — after all I'm not blind. But I was not prepared for news quite that bad — 210 pounds! For roughly a fifteen-year period (age eighteen through thirty-two, or from the beginning of college through assistant professorship) my weight had plateaued between 180 and 185 pounds. But those were the good old days — plenty of time to exercise. If my memory is accurate, I averaged about fourteen hours per week of strenuous exercise during that fifteen-year period. But I must admit that several old friends claim that my estimate is unrealistically low. In any event, it was heaven compared to what's happened to me in the last three years. Most weeks I do nothing — and a padded estimate would be two hours per week of exercise overall. But don't get me wrong, I've tried to exercise regularly. I even succeed for short periods of time. But I always backslide. The time demands on me are just too great.

Something important always comes up to break my exercise schedule — and then I can't get back into it again for months. Doc, you've got to help me."

"What exactly happened three years ago that caused you to stop exercising regularly? Did you stop suddenly, or did you slowly decrease exercising?"

"Well, I was playing basketball and I tore my achilles tendon. I was on crutches for three months, and I couldn't do any strenuous exercise for ten months. During that time my wife and I had our first child and I became involved in the administration of the department. But by the time my leg was healed, I was completely out of the habit of exercising and the number of hours I could spend at work was greatly reduced because of my parenting responsibilities. Plus, I was just busier at work. But my injury does remind me of Bandura's (1982) article on the effect of unexpected events on a life course. In a certain sense, that was a thirty-pound injury! And my problem is compounded now by my personality. I am too impatient and competitive. Instead of slowly getting back into an exercise program, I jump right in, push myself too hard, and wind up hurting myself. Usually my feet or legs will give out — that thirty-pound increase takes its toll on the legs, plus I'm getting older. I could avoid injury by swimming — which I used to do — but frankly, I don't like the way those thirty extra pounds look in a bathing suit."

"Vanity, thy name is human!"

"Point well made, Doc. But that doesn't make it any easier for me to go swimming! However, I will tell you what I did do. Two students, Mary DiGangi and Andy Johnson, wanted to do a volitional study of exercise behavior for people who want to increase exercising. I agreed to be a pilot subject for them. The study ran for 112 consecutive days and was conducted in four phases: baseline; coin toss; choose; and maintenance phases. In the coin toss and choose phases, I tried to exercise as much as I could on half the days, and I tried not to exercise at all on the other half of the days. In the coin phase, the subject flips a coin twenty-eight times and records the results on the last day of the baseline phase. Thus, both the experimenter and subject knew at the outset the exact pattern of "try to exercise" and "try not to exercise" days for the next four weeks in the coin phase. Conversely, in the choose phase, the subject could wait until the day before to decide and record whether the following day would be a "try to exercise" or "try not to exercise" day. Finally, in the maintenance phase I simply tried to maintain a steady daily exercise program. Previous studies (Howard, 1987a; Howard & Conway, 1986; Steibe & Howard, 1986; Howard, Youngs & Siatczynski, 1986; Lazarick, Fishbein, Loiello & Howard, 1986) have documented the ability of this volitional approach to demonstrate the degree to which an individual's behavior is under his or her own control. Figure 3 presents my data for the pilot study. I've also indicated what my weight was at the beginning and end of the pilot study, as well as at the introduction of each phase of the study.

"Those are pretty interesting data, George. You got very little exercise during the baseline period. Then in the coin toss phase you exercised quite a bit more on 'exercise' days than on 'not exercise' days. In fact, the average number of aerobic points (Cooper, 1970) on 'exercise' days (20.28) is about five times the average number of aerobic points on 'not exercise' days (3.96). That seems like pretty good volitional control to me. Then, in the choose phase, you were even more successful. The average aerobic points on 'exercise' days was 21.21, while you never exercised on 'not exercise' days. That's pretty impressive control, I think. Apparently you are in control of how much you exercise."

"Perhaps the choose phase results appear more impressive than they really ought to be. I feel the coin phase was good for me because it urged me to take off from exercising every so often. Those periodic rests probably helped me not to overdo it and injure myself. But let's look more closely at individual days in the choose phase. I started out like a shot — on four of the first five days I chose to exercise and was quite successsful. But on the fifth day I hurt the arch of my foot while playing basketball. I didn't twist it, or anything like that. It just gave out on me. I guess I just pushed too hard too quickly once again. For the next sixteen days I couldn't exercise much (whether designated 'exercise' or 'not exercise' days) because my foot hurt. In the last week of the choose phase I got back into an exercise routine of walking and jogging that my foot could take. In the maintenance phase I kept walking, jogging, and even swimming when my foot began to hurt. In that maintenance phase I simply tried to do a little bit of exercise every day. I feel that I was pretty successful at it."

"I'll say! You lost ten pounds in less than a month of maintenance. Your data in the choose phase

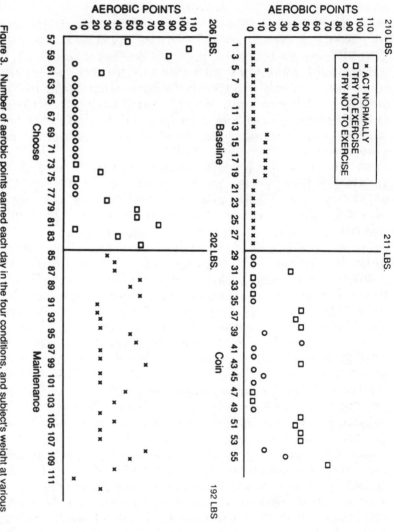

Figure 3. Number of aerobic points earned each day in the four conditions, and subject's weight at various points in the study.

have a very different meaning, when we talk about them as a client and therapist would, than they would appear to have if they were simply analyzed, presented graphically, and reported as a research report. I think data would be richer and more helpful to practitioners like me if researchers discussed their findings with subjects and then not only presented the results in the traditional manner but also presented a 'subject's-eye-view' of why the results came about. Clinicians often assign homework tasks to clients and then get a report from the person not only of how successful they were but also why the client thought he or she was successful or unsuccessful. That's the kind of feedback that helps me to do a better job with my clients.

"George, in spite of the fact that we practitioners hate to correct the logic of you researchers, I feel compelled to note that just because *you* hurt *your* foot doesn't necessarily mean that people generally can't demonstrate greater volition in the choose phase than in the coin phase."

"Good point, Doc! I was concerned that I might infer that I had greater volitional control in the choose phase than in the coin phase, when in reality the data were artifacts of an unexpected injury. But the traditional experiment is not without resources in this regard. Specifically, groups of subjects, rather than simply one subject, are typically run. If the average effect size for volition is greater in the choose phase than in the coin phase, it is extremely implausible that this difference is due to subjects being injured in the choose phase more often than in the coin phase. As I indicated earlier, Mary and Andy conducted this study on thirty-five adults who wished to increase the amount they exercised. The methods employed in the study were identical to my pilot study except that each subject was randomly assigned to either the choose or coin condition in the second phase of their program, with the nonassigned condition becoming that person's third phase. This was done to balance the choose and coin conditions for sequence effects. (Mary and Andy's data can be found in Figure 4.)"

"There are several interesting findings here, George. First, in the choose phase, the 'exercise' days are higher in aerobic points than: a) the 'not exercise'

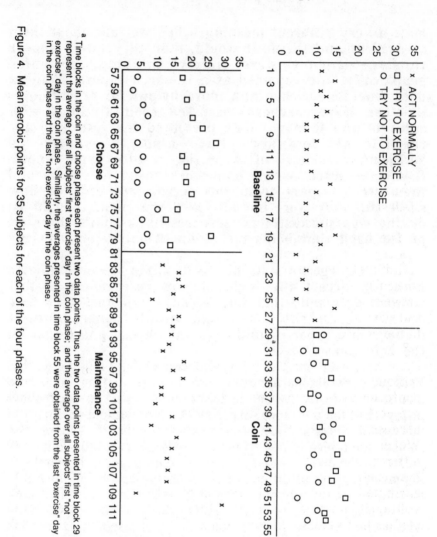

Figure 4. Mean aerobic points for 35 subjects for each of the four phases.

days of the choose phase ($F[1,34] = 37.70$; $p < .001$); and b) the baseline data ($F[1,34] = 10.82$; $p < .01$). Similar comparisons of the 'exercise' days in the coin phase showed their superiority when compared with the 'not exercise' days of the coin phase ($F[1,34] = 7.84$; $p < .01$). When one considers the magnitude of control (i.e., mean 'exercise' days minus mean 'not exercise' days) in the coin versus choose phases, a significant difference also emerges ($F[1,34] = 9.12$; $p < .01$). Thus, subjects demonstrate an impressive ability to separate 'exercise' days from 'not exercise' days in both the coin and choose phases, and are significantly better at separating 'exercise' from 'not exercise' days in the choose phase than in the coin phase."

"That's an important point, Doc. The operational definition I propose of a person's degree of volitional control over a particular behavior is the mean difference on the dependent measure between days on which the person 'tries to perform the behavior' and days on which the person 'tries not to perform the behavior.' In the conceptually cleanest case, days are randomly assigned to 'try to____' or 'try not to____' conditions, as in the coin phase of the study above. To date, there has been only one methodological critique of this operational definition: the problem of subject conformity to the experimenter's commands. That is, perhaps subjects are compelled to obey the experimental instructions because of their need to behave as 'good subjects' (Orne, 1962; Weber & Cook, 1972). If such a critique is valid, then mean differences between conditions would be caused by the pressure of the experimental situation (*a la* Milgram, 1974) and should not be attributed to the subject's power of self-determination, as the volitional interpretation implies. First, let me say that a number of studies (Howard & Conway, 1986, Study 2; Howard, Youngs & Siatczynski, 1988, Study 2; Howard, 1988) have specifically tested the plausibility of the compliance interpretation and found it implausible. Additionally, a quick thought experiment might highlight the compliance explanation's implausibility nicely, and in the process also demonstrate some of the conceptual limitations of our operational definition of volition.

"Imagine that my pilot data on exercise enhancement had been collected in a slightly different manner. Suppose Mary and Andy had chosen a multiple baseline design to test their hypothesis. They not only would have collected exercise data but might also have asked me to track the amount of time I spend reading professional books and journals each day as a second measure, and to record the number of times I slap my thirty-month-old child, Gregory. As you may have guessed: a) I wanted to increase the amount I exercised; b) I was quite satisfied with the amount of time I read, not particularly caring to increase or decrease it; and c) I am ethically opposed to striking my child unless I feel it is absolutely necessary. Well, it's a matter of record that there was good separation between conditions in the coin and choose phases for my exercise data (see Figure 3). I really don't know how the data on reading would have come out: there may or may not have been some evidence of volitional control. But I can assure you that there would not be an iota of separation between 'hit Greg' and 'not hit Greg' days. Now if the separation between 'try to _____' and 'try not to _____' merely reflected a subject's compliance to the experimenter's commands, one would be hard pressed to explain the extreme reactions in the three domains in our thought experiment since the same experimenter gives the three sets of instructions to the same subject at the same point in time.

"But our thought experiment also highlights a potential weakness of our 'try to _____' versus 'try not to _____' operational definition of volition. In many important domains of life I believe that I have volitional control of my actions, and I choose my actions carefully because they have important moral and/or practical implications. In these cases (such as beating my child; lying to friends; ingesting dangerous drugs; etc.) I believe I exert self-control over these actions. However, I believe it would be unwise of me to engage in any of these actions simply to demonstrate that they are under my volitional control.

"Remember that until recently it was impossible unequivocally to attribute the proportion of human behavior to volition (or self-determination, or behavioral freedom, or will, etc.). However, an enormous amount of research findings in psychology are best understood from this active agent, self-determining perspective. But rather than the present operationalization being the final solution to the problem of the empirical specification of the effects of volition in human behavior, it is but a first step toward an adequate solution. From a postpositivist critical multiplist perspective, such as Cook (1985) espouses, scientists must now seek to develop alternative operationalizations of volition. One can assess the degree to which the present operationalization evidences convergent and discriminant validity only when considered simultaneously with differing methods of measuring both volition and other variables located in its purported nomological net of interrelated variables. So we have a good bit of basic instrumentation work yet to be done in this area.

"But instrumentation work also needs to proceed in quite another direction. The methodology for tapping volitional agentic action and testing the limits of behavioral freedom in humans was constructed in such a way as to be scientifically defensible. However, the resulting operationalization of self-determination falls far short of the rich, fully nuanced notion of volition or free will that the humanist has in mind. For example, our operationalization in no way takes into account the individual's interpretation and understanding of his or her actions. The humanist (and also the applied psychologist) longs for a richer specification than the present method affords. Thus, my plans for the future involve developing additional methodologies for studying self-determined action that might be closer to the hearts of humanists and applied psychologists. But, unfortunately, I'm fresh out of bright ideas as to how to accomplish that task. Got any bright ideas I can steal, Doc?"

"No, I don't George, but your point about active agents exerting volitional control in their lives reminds me of an article by Stanley Schachter (1982) in which he claimed that the majority of people who maintain substantial losses in weight don't typically achieve weight losses through formal therapeutic interventions. Rather, they simply initiate weight reduction programs on their own. That finding, plus the data above, suggest that a number of people might wish to lose weight and simply say to themselves something like, 'I'm going to exercise as much as I can.' To the extent they are successful, and our data suggest they often can be successful, that might reflect part of the way in which Schachter's subjects achieved their success. Of course, Schachter's subjects might also have told themselves to 'try to eat less fattening foods' and perhaps they were also successful in volitionally achieving a reduction in caloric intake, which would also help them to lose weight. You simply looked at one factor in the present study — exercise. But I suspect that individuals would be even more successful in volitionally attacking the weight loss problem from as many angles (e.g., diet, exercise) as possible — unless, of course, trying a lot of things leads one to be successful at none of them. But there are no studies on that possibility of which I am aware. That would make an interesting study.

"George, I'm suddenly getting really nervous about the direction in which this conversation is going. It seems both your data and Schachter's findings suggest the importance of self-change, and in the process downplay the importance of psychotherapy. I hope you are not trying to put me out of a job."

"No, Doc, quite the contrary I am trying to help locate the role of the therapist in individualized self-change efforts. I haven't yet told you about the last phase of our study. Remember, the thirty-five subjects represent a heterogeneous group, only a few of whom were considering seeking professional help for their exercise and/or weight control problems. Now our findings indicate that many in this group were able to achieve their goals by volitional, self-intervention efforts. But what about the subjects who were unsuccessful with these self-help approaches? Are they not likely candidates for therapy?

"Mary, Andy, and I identified the fourteen least successful subjects as indicated by the mean difference between their baseline and maintenance aerobic point levels. We randomly selected seven of them to be offered therapy (all seven accepted the offer) while the remaining seven people continued collecting maintenance data (i.e., try to exercise as much as possible) in order to serve as a control group. Mary saw the seven treatment subjects for about one hour a week for four more weeks. She also called them periodically to assess progress, discuss strategies, and encourage them to exercise as much as possible."

"Did it work? Was the therapy successful?"

"It sure was, Doc! Figure 5 presents data on mean aerobic points for the old maintenance phase (now called maintenance phase one) data and treatment phase data (now called maintenance phase two) for the treatment and control group subjects. A significant group effect ($F[1,11] = 8.86$, $p = .013$) was found on maintenance phase two mean aerobic points covaried by mean maintenance phase one aerobic point levels. As can be seen in Figure 5, treatment subjects gained an average of 7.3 daily aerobic points from maintenance phase one to maintenance phase two, whereas control subjects increased only an average of 0.4 daily aerobic points from maintenance phase one to phase two.

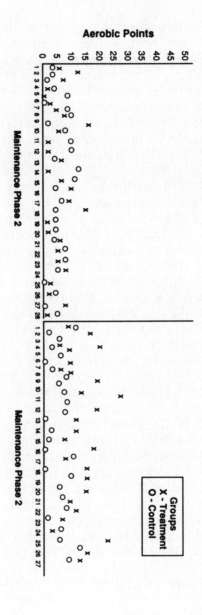

Figure 5. Mean aerobic points for treatment (7 subjects) and control (7 subjects) for the two maintenance phases.

"I'd like to suggest that people can periodically lose their degree of volitional control over some domain of their life (e.g., their weight, smoking, how depressed they feel, etc.). Many are able to reestablish this appropriate degree of control (such as the successful subjects in the early stages of the study above, or Schachter's self-helped subjects). But for whatever reasons, some people are unable to reestablish their normal degree of control, and thus are candidates for professional assistance. My reading of the psychotherapy outcome literature suggests that therapy does indeed work for people interested in obtaining professional help to increase their self-control in most domains, in order to return to normal levels of self-determined action."

"That brings up a favorite topic of mine, George. Do all kinds of therapy work equally well for all problems and all clients? What type of therapy did you use with the treatment subjects in Figure 5, and why, in your opinion, was it successful?"

"There are a slew of thorny problems lurking in those questions, Doc. I am convinced that virtually all kinds of therapy can be successful under the right set of circumstances. As to the curative mechanism involved, it might be the working alliance between therapist and client (Frank, 1961; Patton, 1984), although I don't think anyone knows for certain at this point in time exactly what makes all therapies somewhat effective. The most interesting lead that I've seen recently on this topic is the analysis of the tripartite nature of therapeutic relationships (see Gelso & Carter, 1985) that inevitably develop between therapist and client regardless of the therapeutic approach adopted.

"For the treatment subjects in our exercise study, Mary was highly supportive to all seven subjects. In addition, she was moderately directive with them. By being directive, I mean that she constructed exercise plans with the subjects, called them on the phone periodically to remind them of their plans and to urge them to stick with their programs, and she monitored their progress carefully. In order to understand why we chose this approach to treatment, you must understand our model of therapy. We call it Adaptive Counseling and Therapy (Howard, Nance & Myers, 1986, 1987), or ACT for short. ACT maintains that the most effective therapeutic approaches will be those that correctly match the therapist's style of intervention to the client's level of task readiness. Task readiness is determined by considering the client's competence, confidence, and motivation to improve in the target domain. For convenience, client readiness is thought to range between readiness level #1 (low readiness) through readiness level #4 (high readiness). A client must be almost totally without resources, or severely deficient in one or more component of readiness, to be considered at readiness level #1. On the other hand, clients who are almost ready to terminate successfully, or able to employ self-help procedures (such as clients who were successful in the early phases of our exercise study) would be categorized as readiness level #4. Thus, the subjects in the therapy portion of the exercise study, who were willing to change but unable, were either at readiness levels #2 or #3.

The heart of ACT theory lies in accurately matching the therapist's style (i.e., the exact mix of therapist support and therapist directiveness) with the client's task readiness level. ACT predicts that the matches suggested in Figure 6 will be optimal for the task of moving the client to the next highest level of readiness. Therapy is terminated when the client has achieved the level of self-determination he or she desires (which should also be appropriate for one at his or her present stage and station in life) in the target domain.

Figure 6, presented by Gabbard, Howard & Dunfee (1986), illustrates the following ACT recommendations: therapist style #1 (high directive/low supportive) for readiness level #1 (low task readiness) clients; therapist style #2 (high directive/high supportive) for readiness level #2 (moderately low readiness) clients; therapist style #3 (low directive/high supportive) for readiness level #3 (moderately high readiness) clients; and therapist style #4 (low directive/ low supportive) for readiness level #4 (high readiness) clients. Since our subjects were at readiness levels #3 and #2, high supportive therapist styles were always indicated. The degree of direction the therapist employed was a function of precisely what level of readiness she assessed each individual client to possess. That is, the lower the level of readiness, the more direction the therapist would provide to the therapy. Thus, the positive findings in maintenance phase two speak, in my opinion, to the effectiveness of a supportive therapeutic alliance for clients at levels #2 and #3 of client readiness. Of course, ACT predicts that highly supportive therapist styles would be contraindicated for clients at quite different levels of task readiness."

"That's interesting, George. Am I correct in assuming that the model of human nature that undergirds ACT is that people are potentially capable of volitionally controlling or self-determining their actions in all the important domains of life?"

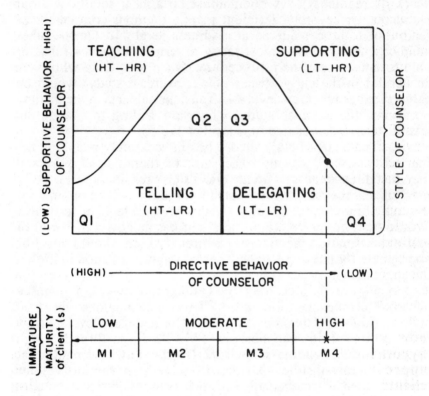

Figure 6. Determining an appropriate therapist style according to client maturity level.

"That's absolutely correct, Doc. Most people handle their lives quite nicely without making use of a therapist. But occasionally, for whatever reasons, each of us can find ourselves a bit out of control in a particular domain, and a little professional help can get us back on a more even keel. Obviously, I am not saying that a person can (or should desire to) *completely* control his or her actions in any domain of life. But what most clients want from therapy is a greater or growing control over their problem. Perfect control is generally impossible because there are many other causal factors at work on us (such as biological, developmental, environmental, psychological, and social factors) that also influence our actions (see Chapter 12). The type of self-control desired in any domain probably should not fall outside the normal range of control that people of a similar stage and state in life exercise. For example, if a client is chronically depressed, the therapeutic goal would not be to eliminate depression completely from the individual's life. Rather, one might strive to have the client experience depression to the degree most people normally do. I mean, do you never feel depressed, Doc? Aren't there unavoidable experiences in life that would (and perhaps even 'should') depress anyone?"

"Since you bring up depression, let me ask you how you would conduct a 'volitional' treatment of a hypothetical depressed person, to be sure I've got this approach straight. After all, I work with depressed clients all the time, but I don't remember ever getting one who simply wanted to exercise more — such people usually go to a health club, not a psychotherapist."

"Fair enough! Let's assume that I encourage this client to monitor his or her mood at two or three points in each day, and that the client produces a reasonable amount of baseline data while I am getting background information and developing the therapeutic relationship. Now let's make the case a bit tougher by assuming that my intuition suggests that direct volitional control (i.e., 'try to feel less depressed' versus 'act normally') would be completely ineffective — so I would bypass it completely. Then I'd ask myself, 'What does the research literature suggest might be the possible causes of depression?' "

"Oh, lots of things might produce depression: disruptive life events (like losing a job, a divorce, a death in the family); biochemical imbalances; overgeneralized negative cognitive schema (as Beck suggests); dysfunctional family systems; lack of

response-contingent reinforcement (as Lewinsohn believes); lifestyle problems (like exercise or diet); or, lastly, a general lifestyle high in punishers and lean in reinforcers might be implicated. Really, almost anything might be a factor in someone being depressed."

"OK! Now my first move would be to view all of your suggestions *not* as causes of depression but as *conditions* that might increase or decrease the client's volitional efforts to become less depressed. Since we've assumed that direct volitional control will be ineffective, I would then test the client's ability volitionally to control the conditions that may aid him or her in his or her volitional efforts to become less depressed. Some of your suggested factors fit nicely into this model (e.g., cognitions, exercise, diet, antidepressant medications, whom one interacts with, etc.) whereas others do not appear to fit (e.g., how would one volitionally control a disruptive life event or a dysfunctional family system?). Suppose we decided to concentrate on two conditions: a) exercise; and b) people with whom the client interacts. The levels of these independent variables might be: a) 'try to exercise' versus 'try not to exercise'; and b) 'try to spend as much time as possible with people you like and as little time as possible with people you dislike' versus 'act normally.' Research designs currently exist that enable one to assess the client's ability volitionally to control the conditions (i.e., how much one exercises, or one's ability to manage how much time he or she spends with certain 'types' of people) and the 'spillover' effect this control has on one's ongoing level of depression. For example, one study (Howard & Conway, 1986, Study 3) considered the ability of forty-five interpersonally shy college students volitionally to increase (both directly and indirectly) the number of heterosexual social interactions in their daily lives. Subjects were able directly to control (i.e., 'try to initiate as many conversations as possible' versus 'act normally') their interactions quite well (effect size: Partial Eta Square = .65). Indirect control of their number of interactions was also achieved. This was accomplished by subjects directly controlling a *condition* related to the desired target behavior, and having this control of a secondary variable 'spill over' to the target dependent measure (i.e., total number of heterosexual social interactions). For example, the effect size for the instruction to spend time in social places on the amount of time actually spent in social places was .46 with a 'spillover' effect size on total interactions of .19. Similarly, the effect size for the instruction to make as many positive self-statements as possible on the number of positive self-statements generated was .32 with a 'spillover' effect size on total interactions of .18. Thus, there is strong evidence that people can modify their behavior by exerting volitional control directly to the target area (as was also the case in the exercise study above), and indirectly by volitionally controlling the conditions asssociated with success in that behavior.

"Thus, my work with the hypothetical depressed clients might include helping them to gain greater volitional control over their overgeneralized negative cognitions, their support structure, their exercise regimen, and perhaps even their diet. I wouldn't work with someone from a family systems perspective, nor would I use antidepressant medications — but that's primarily because of the limitations of my professional background. If family therapy or antidepressant drugs seem indicated, consultation with other professionals or a referral would probably be advised. The volitional perspective sketched here makes many of the same recommendations as does Arnold Lazarus' multimodal therapy (Lazarus, 1976, 1985). I think Lazarus has hit the nail right on the head with his recommendation that therapists initiate work through multiple modes of influence (all directed toward a common multifaceted goal), and that this process be coordinated from a unitary, coherent theoretical perspective. Both Lazarus' multimodal approach and the volitional perspective I've outlined seek to tap multiple channels of influence to help clients regain control over their lives."

"I just had a flash! You see therapy as an aid to individuals in their efforts to reestablish a normal degree of control in some domain where they are a bit out of control. Volition involves being as free as most people to act, think, or feel as one wishes in some domain. That sounds like an issue of personal freedom — or one's range of behavioral flexibility. The title of this chapter ("Reflections on Life, Science, and the role of Therapy in the Pursuit of Happiness") is obviously playing off the phrase 'life, liberty, and the pursuit of happiness.' So are you setting 'science' and 'liberty' at odds with one another?"

"Gee, I'd hate to turn this into a discussion of philosophy of science — but a few basic points might be made. Free will - determinism debates have raged for several millennia. And, in fact, there are several quite different free-will conceptions that have run through these discussions. For example, Mortimer Adler (1958,

1961) sees three different conceptions of freedom. First, free will represents instances where one is not physically coerced to behave in a particular manner. Second, freedom is the state one achieves when one frees himself or herself from internal handicap or weakness, and thus he or she is better able to achieve his or her desired goals. Third, free will involves instances where individuals make choices and act on those choices, *when, in fact, they might have done otherwise.* Our research on volition has nothing to say to Adler's first two meanings of free will. But the research speaks clearly to the third conception. If all other factors had been exactly the same in a particular instance, might a person have actually chosen to behave in a way other than he or she did? Or, as the mechanist suspects, wasn't the person's course of action determined all along — and people's ubiquitous perception of freedom of choice and action merely an illusion? Briefly, I believe that the random assignment of days to conditions (e.g., 'exercise,' 'not exercise'), and the strong evidence (four studies and the 'thought experiment' above) against the 'conformity to the experimenter's commands' interpretation represents the methodological analogue of the conceptual premise 'if all other factors had been exactly the same.' The logic of random assignment is that two groups are created which are equal (on the average) on *all possible* factors save the independent variable (and any variable inadvertently correlated with the independent variable, e.g., conformity). Thus, differences on the dependent variable (e.g., food consumed, amount exercised, etc.) can be unequivocally attributed to the influence of the independent variable, namely, volition. The huge differences we've found on the various dependent measures demonstrate that people can indeed choose to do otherwise, even if all other factors are held the same on the average. Thus, our findings furnish crucial empirical support for what heretofore was only an assumption by the libertarian, or free-will advocate (Howard, 1987b; 1987c). Those data should be welcome support for libertarians who have grown accustomed to having scientific evidence always appear to support their antagonists at the free-will advocates' expense."

"George, I've got a swarm of problems now. I'm sure you have committed a logical error. You just used a deterministic paradigm (the results of scientific investigations) to support an argument for free will. Aren't you contradicting yourself? Besides, I've read somewhere that results of quantum physics have proven the existence of free will."

"You've rubbed me wrong now, Doc. First, I really am bothered by statements like, 'The fact of indeterminacy in quantum physics suggests that there might be free will in humans.' The leap from quantum physics to human free will is too great. The entities that populate the quantum world likely possess enormously different 'natures' than do human beings (i.e., inanimate, subatomic particles versus conscious, active agents). Further, the reasons for believing in quantum indeterminacy are quite technical in nature. Conversely, it seems eminently more reasonable to me to assert the existence of free will in humans based upon the belief in some ontological claims regarding the nature of human beings (e.g., humans possess the power of self-determination), rather than on the outcome of some highly abstract, technical proof. In sum, most scientists would decry a simple translation of findings from quantum mechanics to psychology because there is little *a priori* reason to believe that findings in the quantum realm should have much relevance for explanations of human behavior.

Second, concepts such as indeterminacy, unpredictability, and lack of causality have little or nothing to do with my understanding of self-determination or will. Volitional behavior is predictable, caused behavior. It is such self-determined behavior, as philosophers (e.g., Ferre, 1973; Harré, 1984; Taylor, 1966) and psychologists (e.g., de Charms, 1968; Deci, 1980, Secord, 1984) have claimed, which should be studied more thoroughly by psychologists as an important causal component of a determinant science of human action. Free will (if there is such a capacity) results in determined human action — it does not lead to chance occurrences, uncaused behavior, and the like. My view of volitional behavior as being a self-determined form of caused behavior, amenable to scientific investigation, is designed to get us out of the logical inconsistencies social scientists have been forced to maintain when thinking about 'science' and 'freedom.' For example, Peter Berger (1963), a noted sociologist, handles the problem this way:

> Freedom is not empirically available. More precisely, while freedom may be experienced by us as a certainty along with other empirical certainties, it is not open to demonstration by any scientific methods. . . . Every object of scientific scrutiny is presumed to have an anterior cause. An object, or an event, that *is* its own cause lies outside the scientific universe of discourse. Yet freedom has precisely this character. . . . The

individual who is conscious of his own freedom does not stand outside the world of causality, but rather perceives his own volition as a very special category of cause, different from the other causes that he must reckon with. This difference, however, is not subject to scientific demonstration. . . . There is no way of perceiving freedom, either in oneself or in another being, except through a subjective inner certainty that dissolves as soon as it is attacked with the tools of scientific analysis. (Pp. 122-23).

"To my mind, this represents a very unsatisfactory resolution to the science-freedom problems. Either we have freedom and science is incapable of appreciating this human power; or science can appreciate all human powers, but unfortunately we are not free. This represents an unhappy choice to have to make — but fortunately it is a false dichotomy."

"Well, George, you've now forced me to play the devil's advocate. If self-determination plays as great a role in human behavior as you claim, surely psychological research would have found support for active agency in humans long ago."

"It has, Doc! The evidence for self-determination is all over the place. For example, Mischel and Grusec (1967) show that children who are able to delay gratification employ different cognitive strategies than children who are less able to delay gratification. Presumably, these children would have chosen a different (and less effective) cognitive strategy but chose the more effective approach. Bandura's (1977) self-efficacy theory also hints at volitional aspects of human responding, but it is unclear just how much control any individual has over his/her level of self-efficacy responding. Similarly, Wortman and Brehm's (1974) work on the effects of uncontrollable outcomes; de Charms (1968) insights into personal causation; Deci's (1980) self-determination theory; and some of the cognitive dissonance research (e.g., Wicklund & Brehm, 1976) hint that volitional factors might be involved in these psychological phenomena. One could view the entire choice and decision literature (e.g., Tversky & Kahenman, 1974) as probing volitional behavior (although in such studies the aim is to uncover the developmental, situational, or other types of determinants of choice behavior). In fact, Donald Ford (1987) has successfully reassessed much of the research evidence in various domains of psychology from a self-constructing, active agent perspective. Finally, the first chapter of Bandura (1986) sensitively probes the nature and locus of agency. That is, should human agency be viewed as autonomous agency, interactive agency, or mechanical agency? Skinner believes in mechanical agency and Bandura makes a most compelling case for interactive agency, but no one speaks for autonomous agency; "the notion that humans serve as autonomous agents of their own action has few, if any, serious advocates" (Bandura, 1986, p. 12). That's a shame! Somebody ought to try to sketch a reasonable view of human action that highlights self-determination and autonomy. Unfortunately, the extreme free-will or libertarian position is as obviously false as is Skinner's mechanical agency at the other extreme. If I were a betting man, I'd say Bandura is very close to the truth of the matter in his interactive agency views, although I'd prefer a slightly more autonomous agency flavor to it. But here I'm splitting hairs. Unfortunately, the consensus in psychological research still has been that concepts such as self-determination and/or volitional behavior are either illusory or unscientific (cf. Immergluck, 1964; Skinner, 1971; Lefcourt, 1973)."

"George, correct me if I'm wrong, but didn't Gregory Kimble find evidence that practically all psychologists are determinists and not free willists?"

"Yes and no! He did find that we were all determinists, and his article (Kimble, 1984) highlighted quite nicely the fact that in our roles as psychologists we've all been taught to see the world of human actions through determinist rather than indeterminist (or uncaused, unlawful, unpredictable) spectacles. But the free will advocate is also a determinist who sees the causal power of self-determination (or personal causation) as being paramount in the genesis of human action. Human behavior is lawful, predictable, comprehensible, and controllable for the free willist precisely because of the causal efficacy of self-determination. But Kimble does see evidence for the existence of two cultures in psychology: the scientific and the humanistic. And some theorists see great differences on the free will issue between 'scientists' and 'humanists.' For example, Harré (1984) sees any psychologist's choice as being between a consideration of causal mechanisms and moral orders.

Two images of human psychology compete for our attention. Academic psychologists, particularly those who work in the 'experimental' tradition, make the implicit assumption that men, women and children are high-grade automata, the patterns of whose behavior are thought to obey something very like natural laws. . . . It is assumed that there are programs which control action and the task of psychology is to discover the 'mechanisms' by which they are implemented. Lay folk, clinical psychologists, lawyers, historians and all of those who have to deal in a practical way with human beings tend to think of people as agents struggling to maintain some sort of reasoned order in their lives against a background flux of emotions, inadequate information and the ever-present tides of social pressures.

I shall try to show that the great differences that mark off these ways of thinking about human psychology are not ultimately grounded in a reasoned weighting of the evidence available to any student of human affairs. They turn in the end on unexamined political and moral assumptions. . . . Although these profoundly different ways of interpreting and explaining human thought and action have their origin in preferred linguistic forms rather than any compelling facts of the matter, they do have profoundly different practical consequences. They carry with them very distinctive stances as to the moral, political and clinical problems with which modern people are beset. (P. 4)

"Now if Harré is correct in believing that individuals in the academic (or science) part of psychology tend to adopt a different image of humans than do psychologists who specialize in the application (or practice) part of psychology, then we might obtain a first insight into why we have had such a rocky road in trying to implement the scientist-practitioner model (Gelso, 1979; Howard, 1986b). It is as if we must put on one set of conceptual glasses and view humans solely from a nonagentic vantage point when we take part in science. But when we deal with humans clinically we see them as telic, intending, active agents. Part of what I am trying to point out here is that good research can also be conducted which adopts a volitional, telic, final cause model of humans. Psychologists have long decried the fact that practitioners generally neither produce nor use research evidence in their practices (e.g., Cohen, 1977; Goldman, 1976; Gelso, 1979; Larsen & Nichols,

1972). Gelso (1986) speculates that research studies too often involve clinical methods and experimental procedures that make the findings too far removed from what practitioners and their clients typically experience in practice for the findings to be of much help. 'Experience near' research techniques are offered as a partial solution to the impasse. While the Pepinskys (Pepinsky & Pepinsky, 1954) were perhaps the first to search seriously for such research techniques, Barlow, Hayes, and Nelson (1984) appear to be the best current source for an array of research techniques that create an experience for subjects which is quite near to the actual experience of clients in treatment. Gelso (1986) suggests that practitioners will find the results of 'experience near' studies more helpful and applicable. I'd like to think that the exercise study above is 'experience near' for each of us who struggles daily to maintain an appropriate lifestyle. Further, the last phase of the investigation should be 'experience near' for clinicians whose clients generally have been unsuccessful in establishing self-control in some domain of activity and then seek help in therapy. The view of clients offered in this study is unabashedly telic. However, I believe it is still not only scientifically rigorous but also near to the experience of many potential clients and their therapists. Finally, I wonder if a clinician would find our little dialogue more relevant and applicable to his or her practice of psychology than if we had written up the results in the traditional manner. If the answer is yes, it might simply reflect differing tastes for writing styles. However, it might be due to the fact that the results were presented both idiographically (namely, my personal reactions and interpretation of where the exercise study fit into my life course) and nomothically (you saw the group results also). If that combination of presentations is more helpful for clinicians, it is not unscientific in any way to present findings in that manner."

"**George, since you were willing to take on 'scientific' world-views and 'practitioner' world-views, let me make your life completely miserable by noting that the really difficult problem for many psychologists involves integrating those two world-views with their religious world-views.**"

"Oh, no! What of importance could I possibly say in a few minutes about those heady topics? Allow me first to capitalize upon your personal experiences of some difficult integrations of disparate world-views. Consider the typical applied psychologist. She was probably trained in the scientist-practitioner model. We've all experienced the stresses and strains of that antinomy. I've suggested that one reason for the scientist-practitioner schism might be due to science's antipathy for telic explanations. Since most practitioners operate out of a world-view that sees their clients at least partially in control of their actions (i.e., some form of a telic or active agent model), complete integration with the mechanistic models of humans, underlying much psychological research today, is problematic. By developing a conceptualization of scientific, telic explanations, and fleshing out a corresponding methodology for research into telic human action, one hopes that the previous incommensurability of the 'scientist' and 'practitioner' world-views will have been lessened somewhat.

"But, unfortunately, our 'typical applied psychologist' is also beset by other, related tensions. She might also have a theistic, personal world-view. As we all know, religion with science and religion with therapy have long been uneasy pairs of bedfellows. Can our scientific, telic vision of human action lessen in any way the tensions she might experience between her religious inclinations and her roles as a practitioner or as a scientist?

It seems to me that for many theistic world-views, concepts such as free will, personal responsibility, purpose, intention, culpability, sin, grace, redemption, and so forth play central explanatory roles. Many of those concepts also fit nicely into many person-centered theories of therapy, although the complete integration of religious and clinical beliefs represents a considerable personal challenge for every clinician. But the most intractable antinomy seems to have been between our religious models of humans and the highly mechanistic and positivistic views of humans implicit in the science of psychology thus far in our development as a discipline. The methodology for the scientific study of volition (or self-determination, or behavioral freedom), sketched above, represents a very small step toward a resolution of this last knotty problem.

"In developing a science of active agents, we might now obtain scientific evidence that speaks to the vision of humans implicit in our belief of ourselves and others as religious beings. The initial findings appear to paint a picture of humans who are in large part self-determining, but who are also moved by other causal forces such as biological, environmental, and social factors. That portrait of bounded will, degrees of personal responsibility, and so forth not only meshes well with my understanding of what occurs in the therapeutic encounter but also is compatible with my understanding of my place in the larger scheme of life. Returning for the last time to our hypothetical applied psychologist, it is my hope that a future, fully-developed science of active agents might serve to lessen some of the tensions among her life-as-scientist, life-as-practitioner, and life-as-believer."

"You know, George, isn't it interesting that religion and therapy, which both promote self-determination and subsequent responsibility for one's choices, are such uneasy bedfellows? One would think they'd be allies of one another."

"Yes, you would think that religion and therapy might be allies with one another, but that seems rarely to be the case. I think part of the problem lies in the historical difficulties between science and religion. Since the seventeenth century, science has dealt a series of shocks to Western religious beliefs — and religious leaders have reacted quite negatively (and often inappropriately) to important scientific breakthroughs. For example, religious leaders are now univocal in decrying Pope Urban VIII's treatment of Galileo Galilei because of his publication of the *Dialogue Concerning the Two Chief World Systems*. But it took centuries to achieve consensus among religious leaders on this issue. A science-religion controversy which is still 'hot' is the evolution-creationism dialogue. Now, to my mind, the creationists are simply wrong because they presume that the theory of biological evolution is incompatible with the biblical account of creation and thus one must be right and the other wrong. But many people disagree with my conclusion on that issue (see McMullin, 1985, for an excellent discussion of this issue). So religion's resistance and foot-dragging, in the face of scientific advances in the natural sciences, has created a legacy of animosity. Social scientists fell right into step by seeing religion as the 'opium of the people' (Marx, 1843), or decrying *The Future of an Illusion* (Freud, 1927; religion, of course, was the illusion), even up to contemporary positions that religious leaders generally find distasteful, such as Skinner's (1971) *Beyond Freedom and Dignity*.

Psychologists have seen themselves as rightful heirs in the tradition of great natural scientists whose findings challenge current religious belief, and thus incur the wrath of organized religion. But before we cavalierly assume that we know exactly how history will tell the tale of the social science-religion controversies, let's consider the *quality* of the evidence upon which we are building our antireligion positions. Frankly, I have little or no confidence in the veracity of the observations and interpretations that Marx and Freud employed to make their less-than-complimentary remarks about religion. Skinner, on the other hand, is much more difficult to dismiss. However, it should be obvious from the earlier parts of this conversation that I believe that psychology will soon find ample evidence of behavioral freedom or self-detemination in humans. And if a degree of personal freedom is established, can personal responsibility and human dignity be far behind?

Individuals' religious beliefs and values often become important issues in therapy. As Hans Strupp (1977) has pointed out, therapists must tailor their ministrations to the demands of at least three different interest groups (or publics): the clients themselves; the profession of psychology; and society at large. The wishes of these three publics can sometimes be in conflict with one another, and therapists are often hard-pressed to steer a course of therapeutic action that one or more of these interest groups will not find objectionable. Yet another layer of problems is introduced when the client brings a set of religious beliefs into play in therapy. Of course, the therapist's annoyance with this additional layer of religious value complications is magnified enormously if the therapist himself or herself does not share the client's religious beliefs or value commitments. As with other dimensions (e.g., sex, race, etc.) therapeutic effectiveness might be enhanced when therapists and clients share similar religious beliefs and value commitments.

"But apart from instances of bad therapist-client mismatches on religious beliefs, it appears that the values promulgated in therapy are typically those endorsed by religion. Self-determination, personal responsibility, honesty, concern for the rights of others, and an assertive commitment to what one believes and values are goals endorsed by most therapists and religious leaders. Similarly, most religions can count among their members numerous effective therapists. This suggests that the notions of psychological health and adjustment are sufficiently malleable to fit with an array of religious belief systems.

"Thus, I would note that there appears to be no compelling scientific reasons for psychology to be at odds with organized religions. Further, several important voices within psychology (e.g., Campbell, 1975) have offered cogent arguments as to why psychology might be ill-advised to set itself at odds with cultural institutions like religions and the values they promote. And, finally, the goals of religion and therapy are more often in concert with each other than they are at odds with one another. Thus, I believe we would be well-advised to focus upon the shared interests that unite psychology and religion."

"Oops! I see our fifty minutes is about up. Before we close, let me ask one more question. Remember that speech you gave at the beginning about not exercising because you were so busy? Now that you are exercising regularly, does that mean your schedule is less demanding?"

"Be serious, Doc! I really did think that those time demands represented the primary cause of my inability to make myself exercise. Like you, I am a victim of the cult of psychological, nonagentic mechanisms. We are trained to look for the "causes" of our own, and other people's, behavior. I think we would all do better to heed the wisdom of Shakespeare's claim that 'A man is the cause of his actions.' Time demands, the presence or absence of exercise facilities, physical injuries, societal attitudes toward exercise, and many other factors might be better seen as enabling or restraining conditions that either increase or decrease the likelihood that we will achieve our desired plans, goals, intentions, and so forth. But, clearly, time pressures should not be viewed as 'the cause' of my problem with exercise since the solution to the problem (namely, an hour or two of exercise daily) exacerbates this putative cause greatly. And in spite of this seeming paradox, I happily go on exercising. But you know better than I, Doc, that life involves choices — all of which result in trade-offs. That's what therapy is often all about — namely, helping clients to realize their choices, make helpful decisions, and live with the consequences of those choices."

"One final question, George. What have we been doing here? Have we been engaged in science or in therapy?"

"It's all a matter of money, Doc. If this is research, you should pay me for agreeing to be a subject in this study; if it is a therapy session, I should pay you for letting me talk through these issues. Do you take personal checks?"

"Sorry, George, I don't. Do you take Mastercard?"

Chapter 11

Accuracy Versus Utility in Storytelling

Just the facts, ma'm!
Sergeant Joe Friday, *Dragnet*

Story, n. A narrative, commonly untrue. The truth of the stories here following has however, not been successfully impeached. — Ambrose Bierce, *The Devil's Dictionary*.

"**Do you solemnly swear to tell the Truth, the whole Truth, and nothing but the Truth — So help you God?**"

"I do!"

"**Please state your name and occupation.**"

"Uh, George Howard, psychologist."

"**Professor Howard, I have here a copy of your book entitled** *A Tale of Two Stories*. **I have some serious questions about whether or not you told us the Truth, the whole Truth, and nothing but the Truth in that book. For example, in Chapter 3 you state that your Uncle Bocky visited you at college from Friday morning until Monday evening, approximately a week before his death, under the assumed name of Arnie Palmer. Is that correct?**"

"Well, not exactly. It was a Friday to Monday visit, and I am pretty sure it was a week before his death, but it might have been two weeks. You see, that was almost twenty years ago, and it was a very traumatic period of my life, so I'm not completely certain. And that Arnie Palmer part was just a joke. I mean, that is the sort of thing Bocky was always saying — in fact he probably jokingly called himself Arnie Palmer a couple of dozen times. But if you ask me how he identified himself that Friday morning, I frankly don't remember."

"**Well, Professor Howard, surely you can tell us the name of the student who answered the door. He can then verify that your uncle did, in fact, identify himself as Arnie Palmer.**"

"You gotta be nuts! I can't even remember who my suitemates were that year — let alone who answered the door. Even if I could, it would be a one-in-a-million chance that he would remember the event — let alone the exact wording of my uncle's silly joke. What are you trying to prove, anyway?"

"So, you are unable to corroborate your claim regarding how your uncle introduced himself. Doctor Howard, you might also like to know that I hold here a sworn affidavit from James Hart stating that he has no recollection of ever getting you out of a fight with a stranger from Jersey City. Michael Hart also asserts that he has no recollection that his brother James was present when he..."

"Oh, gimme a break! I distinctly remember Mickey Hart confronting Tony, and I remember that he had some friends with him — it seemed reasonable that Jimmy was one of them — Mickey and Jimmy Hart did almost everything together. Besides, who cares if Jimmy wasn't actually there when. . ."

"Your honor! I intend to show that *A Tale of Two Stories* contains numerous unsupportable claims, and might even be riddled by factual inaccuracies!"

"So is *Cinderella*! Do you intend to prosecute Walt Disney? I would imagine that even a dolt like you might convince a jury that a pumpkin never *really* turned into a beautiful coach, nor did four mice turn into white horses. You missed the whole point of *A Story of George* and *A Story of Science*. I didn't write them so as not to perjure myself, I wrote them in a way that might be illuminating, entertaining, and not at variance with the Truth of what actually occurred. My God! This is nothing but a nuisance *lawsuit*!"

Definition: *Lawsuit, n.* A machine which you go into as a pig and come out as a sausage.

— Ambrose Bierce, *ibid* .

"Let me give you some good *advice*: Tell the jury exactly why you chose to distort the facts to tell your two stories."

Definition: *Advice, n.* The smallest current coin.

— Ambrose Bierce, *ibid.*

"OK! I will! *I believe that we represent the world and our lives to ourselves via stories.* Therefore, psychological research on humans needs to have methods that appreciate and utilize the storied nature of human thought. But, in fact, therapists have a head start on researchers in coming to understand and work with other people's stories, while researchers tend not to get any story information at all about their subjects. To the extent that our thinking proceeds in the form of a narrative, it behooves us to understand the form and structure, possibilities and pitfalls, and characteristics and charms of storytelling.

"The first thing to note is that stories tend to have *points* to them. That is, the reader, listener, or person to whom the story is intended should be able to extract some *moral* from the story. Think about *A Story of George.* What moral emerges from that story? Well, given that the story is unfinished (hopefully, far from finished) the point of the life is still unclear. The meaning would be quite different if I die of a heart attack tomorrow; or if after fifty years of research and writing I come to be known as "Psychology's Newton"; or if my wife Nancy becomes President of the United States; or if (like Dr. Zhivago's experience with the Russian Revolution) the third World War breaks out next month. But while our life's moral is unclear to us while we are living, it is important to reflect frequently upon its possible meanings. ('The life which is unexamined is not worth living,' — Plato.) Further, one creates the meaning of one's life day-by-day, act-by-act, and thought-by-thought. I am urging people to be activists in the creation of meaning in their lives — to take life by the horns and make the best of it that you are able. I believe that we are only partially pawns to genetic/biological factors, social/environmental determinants, and the caprice of random, unintended events. The point is to make the most of what has been given to us — for every advantage brings with it a responsibility.

> — I believe that every right implies a responsibility; every opportunity an obligation; every possession, a duty.
> — J. D. Rockefeller, Jr.
> — For unto whomsoever much is given, of him shall be much required: and to whom men have committed much, of him they will ask the more.
> — Luke 12:48"

"Your honor *must* we be pelted with pious platitudes?"

"Oh shut up you cynical wretch! How does one become a dried-up, withered, old, skeptical *cynic* like you? I'll tell you how it happens. You always expect the worst out of people — and of

---

Definition: *Cynic, n.* A blackguard whose faulty vision sees things as they are, not as they ought to be.
— Ambrose Bierce, *ibid.*

---

life. You persist in telling yourself depressing, negative stories about all that is occurring about you. You have a mean-spirited, suspicious, failure-script. Words like *trust, love, hope, kindness,* and *imagination* are strangers to the phrases you recite to yourself and the stories you choose to believe. You are a lemon of a man!"

"Your honor, I object! Am I to be ridiculed simply because I am not in the *habit* of being a wide-eyed Pollyanna?"

Definition: *Habit, n.* A shackle for the free.
— Ambrose Bierce, *ibid.*

"He's right, your honor. While he's responsible for what he's become, he is not to be ridiculed for it. My apologies. He tends to be a pessimist while I am an optimist — and who really knows how such preferences develop? But let's not consider the etiology of temperament just yet — let's first consider the consequences of optimism. The most important consequence of optimism is that it is enormously energizing and invigorating. Hope is a stimulant! I don't know what your reaction was to *A Story of George*, but I find my life intriguing — I can hardly wait to see how it comes out. It's like a movie that has completely absorbed me. My *mind* is constantly spinning out happy endings,

---

Definition: *Minds, n.* like parachutes. They only function when they are open.
— Sir James Dewar

---

sad endings, bittersweet endings, and commonplace endings (like nothing particularly wonderful occurred, nothing particularly terrible either, he simply grew old and died). But, frankly, I'm excited about my life. It has so many exciting possibilities — I just know one of them is going to pan out beautifully. At times I get so excited about these possibilities that I can't wait to see what's going to happen each day! As a matter of fact, I just looked up at the clock in my office and it's now 4:57 A.M.! Do you want to know why I'm so excited? Because I might have a first draft of this chapter finished by the end of this week.

"Watch out now because I'm going to make three quick points, and I don't have time to drag them out. First, why am I a morning person? Maybe part of it is genetically based — my father was *always* up at 3 or 4 A.M. Maybe it was nurture — when I got up at 5 A.M., it was the only time that I had my father all to myself. We'd have coffee, talk of everything, and get one another ready to meet the day. My father always did manual labor. It was not intrinsically interesting, and I always promised myself to do my best to have an interesting career — not just a job. But sick or well, fair weather or storm, enthused or despondent, my father walked out of that door every weekday at 6 A.M. — without fail. He was a man who knew his duty — and he did it! What do I mean '*was*'? He is now seventy-five and he still works (painting and handiwork) — but the years have taken their toll; he now leaves for work around 7 A.M.! My father never said, 'I love you' to me — he is not a man of words. But, to my ears, his actions have always raised a wonderful din ('Preachers say, Do as I say, not as I do.' — John Selden). How many times I watched him walk out our back door into the dark — leaving me to make of his actions whatever I would. Just a thought — maybe my early-to-rise habits aren't genetically based. My mother has always hated getting up. Dad and the kids always called mom *The Bear:* wake her before 7 A. M. and you could get mauled!

"My second point follows naturally from the first — how do I maintain my early-to-rise habits? Well, one important way is to imagine or fantasize about what I am doing. You've just watched my father walk out our back door to go to work (and *you've also imagined all that that act implies*). I've imagined that scene — and its lessons — many thousands of times. One can also imagine the future ('. . .and so I am pleased to announce that the Leona Tyler award for career achievement in counseling psychology for the year 2018 is awarded to. . .'). Does it matter whether or not it will ever happen? Does it even matter whether or not I 'have a shot at it'? If it spurs me to do my best — to become the best possible psychologist that I can become — who cares? What harm is being done by hoping? Hope is just a little game one chooses to play with oneself — a simple gamble one can take. The up-side in taking the gamble is that you might achieve beyond your own reasonable expectations. Of course there is a possible down-side also — disappointment, frustration, and failure. A word or two should be said about this down-side potential. Remember in *A Story of George* that one of the best parts of my early scholastic lack-of-achievement is that 'failure' doesn't bother me in the least. Why, I've packed more 'failures' into a successful career than you can shake a stick at. You know what I think about failure:

> *Tempare est superare!* ' (To try is to succeed!)
> —State motto of New York;
> 'Tis better to have loved and lost, than never to have loved at all! — Lord Tennyson;
> 'Damn the torpedoes — full speed ahead!' —David Farragut;
> 'You can't make an omelette without breaking eggs!' — Anonymous;
> 'Go for it!'
> — I don't know who said it first;
> 'I'm dying here on the bench, coach — put me in the game!'
> — George Howard (often!).

"OK! You've been more than *patient*. You deserve an explanation for these constant quotes, metaphors, pithy sayings, bits of

---

Definition: *Patience, n.* A minor form of despair, disguised as a virture.   — Ambrose Bierce, *op .cit.*

---

wisdom, and famous phrases. Why is this book literally riddled with them? Well, I think that is how people often think. They tell themselves what appear to be truisms. There is one level of analysis of a life-story where one considers broad themes, overall perspectives, and general orientations. But these meta-story considerations generally are not employed in moments of choice, when one has to act quickly. Do I zig or do I zag? Quick, act! In these numerous instances, we are inclined to reduce a complex situation (which could be understood from many different perspectives) to one (or two) simple issues. We then look to some simple wisdom in guiding our decision. Such aphorisms as: Honesty is the best policy; Never ask a question to which you don't wish to hear the answer; A stitch in time saves nine; and so forth give us a perspective on what might be at issue, and how we should react to it. Of course, it might be that everyone else is a deep, analytical thinker; whereas my wisdom is a mile wide, but only a quip deep. You decide.

"Two philosophers — George Lakoff and Mark Johnson — wrote a brilliant (but unfortunately somewhat dry) book entitled *Metaphors We Live By* that shows the role of brief metaphors in how we view the world and our relationship to it. Metaphors often invite us to see something familiar in terms of its similarity to something else. Consider the metaphors *Time is money* and *Argument is war*. When we conceive of time as if it were like money we think of our time as a limited resource and a valuable commodity and we come to think of 'time' as existing in the same net of interrelationships as does money. Thus, we might hear people say things like:

— How are you *spending* your time these days?
— This person is living on *borrowed* time.
— I need to *budget* my time more wisely.
— This short-cut will *save* us an hour.

Thus, I believe that each of us is constantly striving to make our life sensible (and also to lead happy and productive lives) by using short phrases, metaphors, rules of thumb, and meaningful images to focus our understanding of life and to lend coherence to actions in our daily lives. Persons develop meaning via two distinct (but related) processes. On the macro-level, one creates a coherent life-story or life-script that makes clear where-they-have-been, where-they-are-now, and where-this-all-seems-to-be-going. The second level of meaning is achieved by believing in a set of brief metaphors, rules of thumb, and bits of commonsense wisdom that we reference and employ to construct a meaningful context within which we will decide how we are to proceed.

To make my third point, would you do me the *kindness* of imagining *A Story of George* as if you were a spectator

---

Definition: *Kindness, n.* A brief preface to ten volumes of exaction. — Ambrose Bierce, *ibid.*

---

standing next to the railroad tracks in the railroad station of *The Present*. In Chapter 1 we see George's life approaching as an indistinct form upon the horizon. In Chapters 3 and 5, characteristics of the life become discernible, the life's patterns grow clearer, and, for once, its speed and momentum are roughly calculable. By the beginning of Chapter 7, the train is upon us. As it rushes by its speed takes us aback — the atmosphere of the station is in turmoil from the press of the passing train. The faces of the people on board the train rush by as rapid-fire flashes of pictures. You are struck by 'the blooming, buzzing confusion' of the present, and awed by the mind's capacity to create meaning out of this turmoil. But time is continuous, and the train hurtles into the dark of the future. Almost immediately the distinctness of the train's features begin to recede, and your ability to gauge its speed and direction declines.

Now, turn toward the past again, and replay the image of the train with *A Story of Science*. With the insight of hindsight, we squint to see forerunners of the characteristics of modern science in the work of the early Greeks and Babylonians. As the train of science speeds through the cloudy, dimly lit Middle Ages, little appears to change. Suddenly the train leaps into the sunlight of the Baconian revolution. The characteristics of the machine of science suddenly become blindingly clear. In the few remaining moments before the train reaches you, you are struck by the gathering velocity and tremendous momentum of its bulletlike mass. As it bursts upon the present, you are taken aback by the realization that there are people — like you — on board. As the locomotive rushes into the future you wonder where those people hope to go — and how this train facilitates *their* progress through their many different stories. As science rushes to meet the future, you are torn by conflicting emotions. The thought of all that speed and force hurdling into the darkness chills you, but you realize that the people on the train chose to board the locomotive. They obviously believe that the trip represents an appropriate next step toward each of their imagined futures. We wish the train good luck — but realize that the *future* is always uncertain."

Definition: *Future* , n. That period of time in which our affairs prosper, our friends are true and our happiness is assured.
— Ambrose Bierce, *ibid.*

"Your honor, it is the *responsibility* of the defense to demonstrate the relevance of these fantasies to the case!"

Definition: *Responsibility, n.* A detachable burden, easily shifted
to the shoulders of God, Fate, Fortune, Luck, or one's neighbor.
In the days of astrology it was customary to unload it upon a star.
— Ambrose Bierce, *ibid.*

"I hope the train image helps us to appreciate the notion of
perspective in narratives. You watched my life flash by in *A Story
of George.* While you watched the train as an uninvolved
observer, for me things are different — I am the train! In some
ways, I know the train and the train's trip far better than any of you
possibly could. By the same token, I am enormously interested in
my train successfully completing its appointed rounds. It is a
life-and-death proposition for me. You cared enough to read this
far (*please don't tell me* if you did it because it was a course
requirement). Now what of the factual accuracy of my
autobiographical story? While it is factually accurate, there is
embellishment throughout. You got the highlights (the tedious,
boring, and less meaningful 98 percent of my life was left out).
Further, I cut and pasted the highlights in such a way as to make an
interesting and exciting reading experience for both of us.

"Is *A Story of George* an objective account? No way! It
would take an observer at the station (who then boarded the train
and rode for awhile) to create a more accurate picture. Dag
Hammarskjold disagrees. In his autobiography-like work,
Markings, he claimed 'these entries provide the only true profile
that can be drawn.' While I agree with him that there is a certain
kind of truth to our self-told life stories, their objectivity is limited
by the perspective of the narrator. Crudely put — I let you in on
my self-propaganda! I showed you how I choose to view my life,
in the hope of creating the best future of which I am capable.

It is only by risking our persons from one hour to
another that we live at all. And often enough our
faith beforehand in an uncertified result is the only
thing that makes the result come true.
— William James

It *is not* my job to be completely objective about my life. It
is my job to motivate myself to lead the best possible life of which
I'm capable. This requires that I make my life into an interesting
and exciting story. How else can I get myself motivated to get to

work early each morning? There are a few psychologists on the face of the earth who have had more articles rejected by journals than I — and I still find a way to conduct research and write. Some evenings, when I am responsible for cooking dinner and entertaining our children [Did you really think my freedom to go to work at any ungodly hour of the night represented a free gift? Be serious! That freedom was purchased with the currency of evening responsibilities. Nancy drives a hard — but fair — bargain. I'm glad she does — although at some times I find it hard to appreciate the fairness of it all.] I need an exciting story-line to help me to be the kind of father (and cook) I want to be. But I digress. The bottom line is that I know of no one who has convinced himself or herself that life is pointless, meaningless, or unimportant and then goes on to an exciting and/or important life! Wait a minute, didn't Fredrich Nietzsche do precisely that? But as I said in the first paragraph of *A Story of George*, Nietzsche does not suit my tastes. He's not right; he's not wrong; he's just not for me."

> Man is a rope stretched between the animal and the
> Superman — a rope over an abyss.
> — Friedrich Nietzsche

"Your honor, it is *self-evident* that Dr. Howard is stalling."

Definition: *Self-evident, n.* Evident to one's self and to nobody else. — Ambrose Bierce, *ibid.*

"Undoubtedly, some of you have noted the similarity between autobiographies like mine, and clients' stories, as they are recounted in therapy. Obviously, therapists recognize that there is an important truth conveyed in the client's story. Researchers often operate without this insight — not realizing the deficit they operate under, and thinking that they have the 'best way' of coming to know humans. The therapist (on the other hand) in-dwells in the client's life in order to understand and appreciate how this person experiences life. Therapists do not uncritically believe that what the client recounts is a fair, dispassionate, and objective rendering of the facts of the matter. More often, the tale is best understood as a sympathetic justification of the person's role in (and perspective on) what occurred. The therapist is rarely told the Truth, the whole Truth, and nothing but the Truth. Similarly, therapists often do not attempt to force their clients to face each and every cold, hard fact of what did or did not actually occur in their lives in a completely objective manner. The goals of therapy are more often achieved by taking the person, the story, and the situation as they are, and modifying any (or all) of these components so as to achieve a more satisfactory outcome. The therapist's role in such instances can parallel the craft of a gourmet cook. Chapter 10 gave a hypothetical example of a therapist working with a depressed client. 'Let's see, a dash of Elavil [an antidepressant drug], one half cup of regular physical exercise, slight modification of a self-defeating theme in the client's thought, and two more hours per day of time spent with good friends. That ought to do it!'

"But, happily, with *A Story of Science* I was able to tell an objective, accurate story, since it wasn't a story about me. Be serious, George! What are the chances that the history of science will come barreling straight through your particular interest area? Not likely! Well, it is equally unlikely that the *real Story of Science* will come crashing through my research on self-determination and how humans achieve meaningfulness in their lives via storytelling. Once again we must consider the perspective of the storyteller. In *A Story of Science*, I am not the train, I am more like a passenger on the train. I just hope the train winds up where I would like it to go. But it is my experience that many scientists see their own research as being 'on the cutting edge' of science. As I mentioned earlier, this represents, in part, a motivational strategy. Science is tiring, difficult work, often pursued with few extrinsic rewards. But scientists typically believe in the rightness or truthfulness of their ideas, and often imagine how greatly their field would be changed if their experimental demonstrations were to work out as well as they imagine. So my story of a human science developing in the future should not be seen as a prediction of what might occur, but rather a *hope* of what will occur. Why do I hope for

---

Definition: *Hope, n.* Desire and expectation rolled into one.
— Ambrose Bierce, *ibid.*

(and work toward) a science of self-determination with storytelling as an important mechanism whereby such volitional control is achieved? Why would I prefer such an image of humans to one that emphasized, for example, environmental determinism, some form of biological reductionism, and so forth? In part, it is because I believe that people *are* self-determining active agents. But, more important, I can see where I might have something to offer in moving forward a self-determining, scientific conception of human action. Had I a novel insight into the way that environments coerce human action, I might see humans as being more mechanistically determined than I now do. But, for now, radical situationism and models of biological reduction will have to get along without the benefit of my insight — and they will, I wager.

   "I'll close by explaining why I included all those *cynical* definitions throughout this chapter. Joseph Rychlak has long held

---

Cynic, n. A man who knows the price of everything, and the value of nothing.
                                                          — Oscar Wilde

---

that human thought proceeds dialectically and oppositionally. I say 'white' and you naturally think 'black.' I mention 'free will' and you think of 'mechanistic determinism.' My point is that even as I tell my story to myself, there is another part of me that is cynical and skeptical about my own construal of events. This is an important self-correcting, self-critical power that humans possess. Writers are particularly prone to hear imaginary readers object to what they are saying — or simply protesting that their choice of a particular word renders the precise meaning unclear. A person's stream of consciousness more often resembles a dialogue rather than a monologue. This self-critical capacity is important, for while it is helpful to use a story as a self-motivation strategy, *one would never want to be completely taken-in by one's own self-propaganda.* The cynic in you is painfully aware that words conceal as much as they reveal—that is why my cynical side provides a few definitions of words in this chapter. Thus while we construct, live in, and (to a certain extent) 'believe in' our story, most people can maintain some detachment from (and critical stance toward) their self-motivation strategies and construals of the world. Am I right? Or am I just more of a 'split personality' than the rest of you? You be the judge. And with that, your honor, I rest my case."

Chapter 12

A Model of Humans as Storytelling, Active Agents

What a piece of work is man!

— William Shakespeare

Today in class I heard myself saying some things that were shocking. I usually know what I will say in class, but in my own defense, today I was under a lot of pressure. The final assignment for my honors social science course was to write an essay on "What is distinctive about a social science?" As their instructor, I was to be a resource in helping them to puzzle through this thorny problem. And as humans are wont to do, the students were sorely testing the limits of this resource. They were relentless — as bright, motivated students (under the gun of a writing assignment) often are. You see, their problem was to pull together what appeared to be only tangentially related approaches to understanding social action, such as psychology, political science, economics, anthropology, and sociology.

It quickly became clear that the students' difficulty lay in integrating what they had learned throughout the semester in a manner that made sense. I decided that a quick exercise in how one might integrate what appear to be disparate lines of thought in a science might be helpful. Being a psychologist, I chose as an example that which I know best — psychology. I'm telling you this story because it traces a formal model of human action from this storytelling, self-determining, active agent. Further, it also quickly reviews some of the points made earlier in this book. I hope this exercise serves to integrate some of the themes traced in this book — and besides, anything worth saying is worth saying twice. So here's how the class went.

"Let me give you a lesson in the art of integrating seemingly incompatible lines of thought. Doing so might help you with your writing assignment. You see, psychology is no different from any other science. In order to understand something, you first try to simplify it. Strip away distracting elements, the irrelevant, the peripheral, and get to the heart of the issue. Then you work with the central mechanism, the core entities, the driving parts of the thing you are studying until you really know them well. For example, we read a little bit of Freud about a month ago. What were the core elements or constructs in his view of humans? Mary, what do you think?"

"Well, he thought there are biologically based psychological forces in a person's id that are in conflict with a person's conscience or superego. And this third entity in people, the ego, kind of negotiates or referees the battles between the id and superego. But some of these conflicts go on unconsciously, and so we try to understand behavior we can see (like the neurotic behaviors Freud's patients were exhibiting) as caused by these unconscious conflicts."

"Exactly! Now many of Freud's followers couldn't buy a view of humans that was that simple. People such as Carl Jung, Otto Rank, and Karen Horney, who basically agreed with Freud's core position about the unconscious determination of behavior, pressed for a more sophisticated view of human action. They argued for the importance of a particular event in a person's life (such as Rank's 'birth trauma'), factors beyond the individual (such as Jung's 'collective unconscious'), and so forth. To the end, Freud tried to keep his theory simple, pure, and uncluttered by these additional factors. But contemporary psychologists, who see themselves as intellectually directly descended from Freud (usually referred to as psychodynamic psychologists), try to consider a broad array of factors in explaining human action. However, the thread that ties all psychodynamic types together is their view of the importance of intrapsychic factors in human behavior. Mike, you have a question?"

"Is B. F. Skinner a psychodynamic psychologist?"

"Bite your tongue, fellow! Nothing could be farther from the truth. Skinner sees human behavior in terms of the rewards and punishments that follow our actions. Behaviors that tend to be followed by a reinforcing set of circumstances (usually rewarding, pleasant, or satisfying states of affairs) will increase in frequency over time. So if you wish to understand a person's actions, look at his or her current set of circumstances, and the individual's prior learning history in similar situations, and you will be able to understand his or her behavior. For example, if you hoot, whistle, and scream in this class, or in Sacred Heart Cathedral, you are probably going to get in trouble. But at a Grateful Dead concert or at a football game — hoot-on — such behavior is appropriate and even reinforced. So, according to Skinner, present reinforcement and punishment circumstances (or contingencies) control our behavior. But everyone doesn't act exactly alike in the same circumstances. This is because we each have different learning histories. Some of you were often punished for giving answers in class in the past, while others were generally reinforced. Patricia?"

"Does knowing the right answer have anything to do with who puts her hand up?"

"Considering this class, I have my doubts. Come on! Stop the yelling! Settle down! I'll get serious again. As happened to Freud, over time other behaviorists forced Skinner to expand the scope of his central theory. With regard to your question, Pat, Michael Mahoney, Carl Thoresen, Albert Ellis, and other theorists forced Skinner to consider closely what the person is thinking about in his or her present situation as an important element in explaining the person's behavior. For example, if one of you were to do something that annoyed me and I berated you in class, most of you would find my abuse punishing, and would be less likely to do whatever you did again. But consider the unlikely event (I hope!) that one of you — Mr. X — hates my guts. Mr. X does something really out of line, and I berate him for it. Mr. X thinks, "Great, I really got that joker's goat!' For him my abuse was reinforcing, and might serve to increase his acting out in class in the future. We call this phenomenon 'obtaining secondary gain.' Even more interestingly, consider this scenario. Mr. X also has his eye on Ms. Y and he knows that she likes me even less that he does. If he disrupts class not only does he get secondary gain from it, but he also believes his action will win him points with Ms. Y — and he is *highly* motivated to win points with Ms. Y."

"Excuse me, Dr. Howard. Is the point you are making that a good teacher should do *everything* in his or her power to stay in his or her students' good graces in order to avoid a situation where they might obtain secondary gain from inappropriate actions? I was thinking about the term paper assignment and wondered if you might see important educational benefits in reducing the scope of that, perhaps overly ambitious, assignment."

"Tim, I'm thrilled that you profited so thoroughly from our discussions of Karl Marx and his treatment of 'class interests.' But getting back to behaviorism, the thread that ties behaviorists together is that it is the consequences of our actions that determine what we will do in the future. Yes, Betty, you have something to say?"

"In the *Notre Dame Magazine* a while back they had an article that suggested that advances in the scientific understanding of the biochemistry of behavior would eventually lead to pharmacological methods of curing all psychological disorders, enhancing memory, curing criminals, and an incredible number of other human problems. What do you think of those claims?"

"Good point, Betty. I thought it was an incredibly interesting, but slightly misleading, article. But to understand my reaction, we must analyze the article from several perspectives. Remember when you read Freud's *Psychopathology of Everyday Life*? Your reaction was 'Ridiculous! He tries to explain everything with a few simple constructs.' Or remember your reaction to Milton Friedman's monetarist view of inflation in the economy? 'Probably too simple,' you concluded when you also considered John Maynard Keynes' fiscalist position and Arthur Laffer's supply side approach. Rarely (if ever) can social scientists furnish a complete and satisfactory explanation of complex human behavior with one, or only a few, basic principles. Later I'll flesh out why, in my opinion, this must always be the case. For now, suffice it to say that some very interesting work is being done in psychopharmacology which will hopefully contribute to human welfare in the future. But, in my opinion, the important human problems that psychology faces will not be improved appreciably by fine-tuning people's biochemical balance. Drugs undoubtedly influence our moods, our thinking, and our actions. This is so because of our material natures. However, I believe that the potential benefits of biopsychology are currently being oversold. But, as suggested earlier, the outlandishly optimistic claims of the author of that article probably represent something of a rhetorical device that scientists have long used to reenergize themselves to tackle the enormously difficult and tiring work involved in converting a research idea into a scientifically demonstrated reality. Question, Paul?"

"But if they could come up with a pill that could totally cure psychological disorders, wouldn't that prove Freud wrong?"

"Well, if that were to happen, it would certainly cause all psychologists, who hold models of humans that emphasize psychological phenomena more than biological phenomena, to scurry back to the drawing board and rethink the model of humans that is presupposed in their approach to understanding human behavior. But let's slow down a bit here. I introduced a number of new ideas in that last sentence very quickly, and I must explain them clearly or risk some of you not understanding my position. First of all, I think it is enormously unlikely that anything like the pill you suggested will ever be found. At this point what we have found are some chemical agents that are rather helpful in combating some of the symptoms of emotional difficulties. But this is a far cry from using drugs to effect a cure of the fundamental causes of psychological problems.

"But the more interesting issue at stake here involves the relationship between a scientist's model of humans and how that scientist will interpret the results of his or her studies. Let me demonstrate this by some simple diagrams. Assume in these diagrams that the area inside the square represents a person's behavior, and the circles represent how much a particular class of potential causal factors (such as psychodynamic forces, biological influences, environmental contingencies, societal influences, astrological influences, etc.) actually influence that person's action. Now in Figure 5 we'll crudely try to diagram Freud's view of the causes of human behavior.

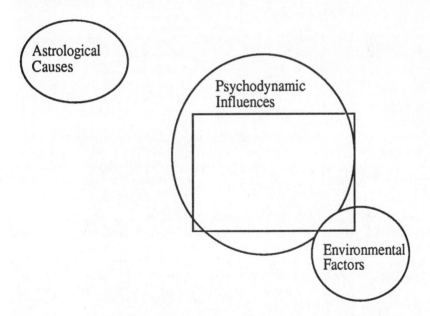

Figure 7: Rough schematic drawing of Freud's view of causation in human behavior.

"You can see in Figure 7 that psychodynamic factors are overwhelmingly responsible for a person's actions (diagrammatically, they cover the greatest area of the box). Environmental influences have a slight role in behavior, as Freud recognized their role as triggering mechanisms for the expression of repressed intrapsychic conflicts — thus, environmental factors overlap slightly with the box. To my knowledge, Freud did not believe that astrological forces played any role in human behavior — thus, no overlap with the box. In Figure 8 we will depict a fictitious psychologist who is a bit more balanced than was Freud in his or her view of human nature. This psychologist might be

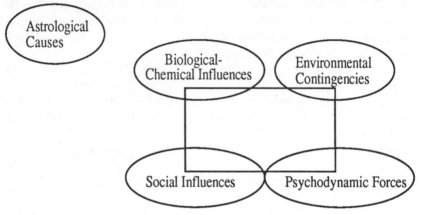

Figure 8: An atheoretical, eclectic view of causality in human behavior.

described as a thorough eclectic who takes no strong position (except an aversion to astrological influences) on the question of what makes people tick. This individual sees reason to believe that psychodynamics, environmental contingencies, societal influences (such as social class, societal institutions, etc.), and biological-chemical factors each play a role in the genesis of behavior. And so you can see that each of us has an implicit set of beliefs regarding the wellsprings of human behavior. But beware, I have employed a number of simplifying strategies in constructing this simplistic picture of the real situation. I have implied that one can easily assign a potential cause of human behavior to one and only one domain of influence, which is not really true. For example, remember from your reading that Freud considered his drives to be biologically based. So which are they — biological or psychodynamic in nature? Do you want to say something, Tom?"

"What about psychic forces like E.S.P., psychokinesis, and that stuff? Do they influence our behavior?"

"I haven't a clue. Mary?"

"What about religion? What effect does that have on us?"

"I'm not a theologian. I haven't a clue there, either."

"Wait a minute!! That's a cop-out. We didn't come to

Notre Dame for the football team. Part of being at a Catholic university is that we will get at least an honest effort at integrating what we learn with our beliefs."

"You're right, Mary. I'm sorry. I try to confine my comments in class to areas where I feel my training gives me some special expertise. I certainly don't want to waste anyone's time or patience with ill-formed or stupid ideas. Please excuse me if my grasp of theological issues is naive or unenlightening. I'll give it my best shot. Please bear with me.

"One of the things I learned from my study of calculus is that it is often enlightening to push things to their extremes. You know, what is the value of a function as X approaches zero? What is the function's value as X approaches infinity? Analogously, how would we characterize the situation where our circle for spiritual causes completely dominates a person's box to the complete exclusion of environmental, psychodynamic, biological, and all other potential influences? That would be something like the case of predestination, wouldn't it? God set up everything, and so anything that happens is simply God's will. Conversely, if the spiritual domain does not overlap with the box at all, then it is like astrology in our previous examples. What would that mean? Well it could mean that there is no spiritual domain, and hence it couldn't possibly influence human action. Or perhaps the spiritual domain really exists, but God chooses to leave human affairs totally alone. That also would show up in our diagram as no overlap between the spiritual circle and the square. Fred?"

"What do most psychologists think? How much overlap is there between the spiritual circle and the box?"

"I have two answers to that question. First, I honestly believe that question is more appropriately answered by theologians than by psychologists. As I structured the problem, I believe that questions about the amount of overlap are simply outside of the area of psychologists' competence. We have no special insight to offer. Second, history tells us that psychology and religion have been, at best, uneasy bedfellows. For example, Freud's thoughts on religion are in a book entitled *The Future of An Illusion.* As you might have guessed, in that book, religion was the illusion. But it's my impression that all of the social sciences have historically had a rather uneasy relationship with religious thought. Remember, for example, in your readings, Marx called religion the 'opiate of the masses.' Hardly a view that will win you friends in religious circles."

"Well, professor, what do *you* think is the amount of

overlap between the spiritual circle and the box in your model?"

"I'd like to answer that question, but I don't think you would understand my answer yet."

"Try us; after all, we are honor students. Witness the outrageously difficult writing assignments you have been giving us!"

"*Touché!* But I wasn't questioning your intellectual capabilities. I simply meant that I couldn't present my view yet because I haven't specified what, in my view, is the most critical causal element in human behavior. Would anyone like to take a wild guess at what that element might be? Nancy?"

"Free will?"

"My God, that's right! How did you know that?"

"A woman's intuition? Maybe my guardian angel whispered it to me? Just a lucky guess? Who knows? Maybe it's a mystery?"

"Maybe. Who knows? Anyway, free will isn't a totally correct label for my central explanatory construct in human behavior, but it is remarkably close. Let me say that a large number of psychological theorists have speculated about a number of human powers such as volition, self-determination, self-actualization, personal constructs, autonomy, active agency, self-control, free will, and many more. I associate names of psychologists such as Carl Rogers, Abraham Maslow, Gordon Allport, Paul Secord, Bill Tageson, and George Kelly, as well as philosophers like Rom Harré, Charles Taylor, Larry Wright, and Stephen Toulmin as speaking to the human powers that I feel are central to what it means to be a human. Terms such as *humanistic, teleogical, person-centered, growth-oriented,* and *action theorist* are at times given to subsets of these thinkers, but I would be surprised if any one of them would agree that all of the labels I just mentioned are descriptive of their thinking. In its most blatant form, my position might be characterized as follows: If you want to know why a person behaved in a particular manner, ask him or her! The answer may sometimes be incomplete, or uninformed, or even purposely misleading. But in leaving out an individual's account of why he or she behaved as he or she did, we lose access to what, in my opinion, is the central human capacity in the formation of human action. In contradistinction to the belief of most psychologists today, I believe that it is not the past or the present that is primarily responsible for human behavior, but rather it is the future, as imagined by that individual, that is crucial in how we form our actions. Schematically, my view of the wellsprings of human action is depicted in Figure 9.

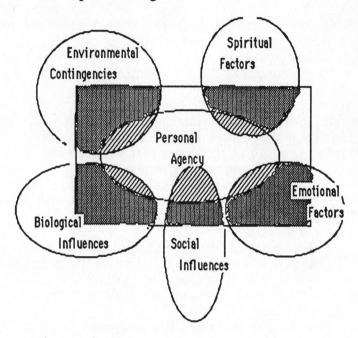

Figure 9: Causal factors in human action.

For lack of a better term, let us refer to the core construct of human action, which was loosely described above, as *the self*. Figure 7 locates the self at the center of human behavior. As can be seen from the diagram, biological, social, environmental, and psychodynamic influences can exert their influences independently of the self (the shaded areas). But from this perspective, other potential influences (such as environment, biology, etc.) of human behavior sometimes (perhaps often!) achieve their effects in the formation of human action through the action of the self (the striped areas). This conceptual move stands the conventional wisdom in psychology on its head. For example, let me assure you that there is a very close relationship between the amount of coffee I drink at the office and how much writing I get done. Any biologically oriented psychologist would immediately begin to talk about the effects that the stimulant caffeine has on my activity level, and how this facilitates my writing. Now that analysis is not totally incorrect. It simply misses the most interesting aspect of the phenomenon. Let me assure you that when I decide to write, I choose to drink a good bit of coffee in order to facilitate my desired action. How about an example involving environmental contingencies? I also get a lot more writing done when I leave my office door closed than when it is open. Environmental psychologists would jump at this relationship and maintain that I am under the control of this environmental condition. But that's not the most important thing going on here. I'm altering the environment (by closing the door, or turning off the stereo, or whatever) in order to help myself meet my goals. Or as Albert Ellis maintains regarding the genesis of our emotions: our emotions are primarily the result of the things that we keep choosing to tell ourselves. Yes, Ed, you have a question?"

"Not a question really; I think I understand what you are saying, and I'd like to take a shot at how you will handle the relationship between spiritual factors and the self."

"Go for it, Ed!"

"Insofar as one believes in a spiritual dimension to his or her life, the person actually brings a spiritual reality into existence in his or her life. And in so doing, the spiritual dimension becomes a causally efficacious entity in the formation of that person's action. Something like that?"

"Something like that. But remember that there is a far stronger claim that can be made (and actually is quite frequently made) about the real existence of a spiritual reality that is independent of whether or not people choose to believe in its existence. But here I can't see where psychologists have anything special to say. We each simply have our own opinion on this topic. Bob, you look puzzled."

"What is this *self* entity, anyway?"

"You, Bob! It's *you* who is acting upon the world for your own purposes, plans, and so forth. But I know that the self is a slippery, nebulous term. I could have called it 'mind,' or 'ego,' or 'consciousness,' or 'personhood,' or any other term. But, in my opinion, 'personal agency' or 'self-determination' comes the closest to the human power (or capacity) I am trying to describe.

"Now one might wonder exactly how this ability to self-determine is achieved by a person. Well, I'm now writing a rather speculative book entitled *A Tale of Two Stories* that suggests that at its core, human thought is storytelling. Some stories allow people to have greater control over their lives, whereas other stories picture people as pawns to other powerful forces in their lives. In believing one cannot self-determine, a person actually brings about (or creates) the reality that he or she cannot self-determine. As

Heraclitus pointed out over two millenia ago, 'one must hope, for one will not find the unhoped for.' That is, it is one's hope that leads one to the discovery of something. *Some stories are simply more 'hopeful' than others.* And certain people, like therapists, ministers, and so forth, are trained to discriminate 'Winner' from 'Loser' stories, and to help the person to retell (or reconceptualize) the story in a way that is more hopeful. Of course, these retold stories must be realistic — but a good story will have someone striving for goals that represent both desirable and possible goods, but which are as yet unrealized. Claire, is your hand raised?"

"Well, psychology is a science, isn't it? What does research have to say about self-determination in human action?

"Almost nothing, Claire!"

"Come on, Doctor Howard. There must be thousands, maybe hundreds of thousands, of studies in psychology. None of them test whether personal agency is an integral part of the formation of behavior?"

"I am so glad you all had Ernan McMullin for your philosophy of science course. Anyone without a good grasp of the essence of science will find it tough sledding from here on out. Also, because of time constraints, I'll need to simplify complex arguments and summarize large bodies of literature. I have published some articles on these topics recently, and I'd be happy to let you read them if you need the complete arguments to be satisfied that you fully understand the moves I make. So let's jump right in.

"Kenneth Gergen claims, 'Observers of the sciences frequently comment on what they take to be a deep and pervasive discontent with the outcomes of traditional research pursuits. With increasing outspokenness, investigators of high visibility and lengthy research experience have begun to raise sobering questions concerning the promise of traditional science' (Gergen, 1982, p. 190). Gergen then documents his point by citing eighty-five recent books and professional articles dealing with this discontent. I know of at least a dozen additional critiques that Gergen failed to cite. But why this extensive airing of my discipline's dirty linen? Simply because psychologists, when threatened, are often tempted to employ defensive strategies such as denial ('The problem isn't really that serious!') or obfuscation (as Koch suggests, usually couched in scientistic terminology with a thick coating of statistical jargon). Don't be misled. With precious few exceptions, research in most content domains of psychology is in some degree of trouble. But after all, psychologists are human beings also, so why shouldn't they defend their professional domains? Why shouldn't they have access to the same protective strategies also employed by other humans? The problem is that defensive attitudes do not get the deficiencies in our current research practices remedied. So what do I have to offer toward a solution? Mike, you have a question?"

"Hurry! We're running out of time! First, unless I miss my guess, you're going to suggest that research in psychology that includes your self-determination construct will furnish a superior explanation of human action than research as it is currently practiced. Are you suggesting that psychological research currently only deals with the influence of environmental, biological, psychodynamic, and social influences on human behavior? Second, are you saying that nobody does research on the role of personal agency in human action? I can't for an instant believe that is true!"

"You're a sharp cookie, Mike. You've guessed correctly where I am heading. But with regard to your second point, I'm not nearly as negative on psychologists' research efforts to date as you think. More on that later. However, I do think psychological research, as currently practiced, often strives to furnish a completely mechanistic account of human action. Joseph Rychlak makes the point this way:

> Most of us can describe in general terms how our stomach or heart works, but we haven't the foggiest notion of how to describe the workings of our free will. If we turn to scientific texts we are sure to be disappointed because the going assumption in science is that we are *not* really free but mechanistically determined. Even though there is growing scientific evidence in support of a free will conception of human behavior, the public never gets this message because such findings are put through a mechanistic wringer before they are presented to us as "facts. (Rychlak, 1979, p.vii)

Remember, Skinner has a particular view of what represents the *proper form* of any scientific explanation, and seemingly indeterminate constructs like 'free will' simply don't fit that view. Thus, in his opinion they're out! Plus, I bet his personal belief is that human behavior *is* totally determined by personal historical factors interacting with current environmental contingencies. Unless I miss my guess, all of the world looks pretty coherent through Skinner's eyes. Question, Fred?"

"You bet! How can someone who doesn't believe in freedom, autonomy, and human dignity be a Catholic? How do you behaviorists reconcile your professional views with your religious convictions?"

"Fred, I hope you haven't been asleep for most of this class. I am a psychologist! I am anything but a behaviorist! However, you do raise a good point. First, Skinner does not speak for all behaviorists. He is an extremist. Second, there are some good behaviorists who are also good Catholics. But none of them has ever explained to me exactly how they integrate their religious and scientific belief systems. So I guess we'll just have to ask them how they manage it, won't we? Third, many professionals make no effort to integrate their professional views with their personal lives. They simply see them as separate domains. Speaking for myself, it never occurred to me that my personal agency model wouldn't be completely compatible with my beliefs as a Catholic. But now that I think about it, I'm going to run it past Father Burrell and Father Dunne. Those guys have strong opinions about everything. It will be fun! Thanks for the suggestion. Mike, you are nervously eyeing the clock again."

"I am! I'd hate to miss the punch line to this story because the bell rang. Your suggestion that Skinner has a narrow view of the types of explanations that are appropriate for science really got me thinking about what sort of explanation your attribution of causal force to this personal agency construct would represent. Unless I misunderstand my philosophy classes, it's a teleological explanation of sorts, isn't it?"

"You've read my mind. And here's the bottom line: teleological explanations have a bad reputation in science, in general, *and research in psychology has traditionally been designed so as to systematically exclude them altogether!* I believe that fact has had an enormous amount to do with the dissatisfaction many feel with what psychological research has accomplished thus far. But let me flesh out that point in a bit more detail. Remember Jacob Cohen's (1977) point that even under the best of circumstances, psychological research seems to have an effective upper limit of prediction of about 25 percent to 33 percent of the variance in human behavior? Well, if I'm right, and much of human action is volitional in nature (i.e., a reflection of this capacity of humans for personal agency), then variance due to volition inappropriately gets thrown into the pool of unexplained variance, along with other sources of variance that rightfully belong in this pool of unexplained variance (such as error in measurement, etc.). If personal agency accounts for a huge portion of human action, then our studies are doomed to account for a minor portion of the variance in human behavior, *even if we understood all the nonvolitional causes of the particular behavior* under study, and were able to measure all constructs perfectly! And those are really big 'ifs.' I see Madalene has a question."

"I'm afraid you lost me. What are teleological explanations? And why don't scientists like them?"

"I'm sorry. I'll try to be clearer. Simply stated, a teleological explanation is generally one that appeals to a purpose, an intention, or a reason. Sometimes an appeal to a plan or a strategy can also represent a teleological explanation. With regard to your second question, it requires a bit of an interpretation of some of the history of science in order to understand it. In my opinion, psychology adopted its conception of what constituted appropriate types of scientific explanations from the natural sciences. During the seventeenth century, the natural sciences began systematically to exclude teleological accounts as explanations. Until that time, it was not uncommon for scientists to anthropomorphize their subject matters and explain their behavior via teleological accounts. But given the enormous success of the mechanistic, deterministic Newtonian paradigm in physics and the other natural sciences, some scientists and philosophers of science overgeneralized (in my opinion) the importance of all scientific explanations being nontelic in nature. Claire, you have a question?"

"So why don't psychologists run some studies to test whether self-determination is an important cause of human behavior?"

"Good idea! But it's not quite that simple. Scientists know that good theories are those that can predict the outcomes of experiments the best and. . ."

"Oh no! You're wrong there, professor! Father McMullin says that the task of choosing among various theoretical accounts in science is an enormously complex enterprise. Appeals to criteria other than predictive accuracy, such as internal consistency, coherence, fertility, unity, and simplicity are often. . ."

"UNCLE!! UNCLE!! You and Professor McMullin are undoubtedly correct, and I am wrong. Now we know why he is an endowed chair and I'm not. As I should have said, for the working scientist, perhaps the single most important criterion in choosing among competing explanations of a particular phenomenon is predictive accuracy. Is that better now? But here is the rub: For every other science on the face of earth, the prediction and control that served as the warrant for enhanced understanding *was prediction and/or control of the phenomenon by the scientist, not by the object of investigation.* Scientists predicted the behavior of planets, or chemicals, or falling bodies in their studies. The planets, chemicals, or falling bodies didn't predict their own behaviors. But personal agency, of its very nature, implies prediction and/or control by the behaving agent, not the scientist. To make a long story really short, all the existent models of experimentation were inadequate to the task of assessing the portion of variance in human behavior that could logically be attributed to personal agency. Important technical modifications, in the manner in which studies are conducted, needed to be devised and refined. I've got a paper totally devoted to those problems and solutions, if anyone is interested in considering those issues closely. Tim?"

"Thank God, you are *finally* ready to run some studies! Quick, tell me. Do people really have volitional control of their behavior?"

"*Touché!* Turnabout is fair play, Tim. You're using sarcasm on me. Of course humans can behave volitionally! If our studies had suggested that they couldn't act volitionally, we would have suspected the inadequacy of the technical modifications we had made. I keep forgetting that because of your philosophy of science background, you people have a sophisticated understanding of the role of evidence in science. Well, as it turns out, the evidence shows that people *do* in fact behave volitionally. What was shocking was how perfectly the evidence fit with what one would logically predict. For example, shy people in fact demonstrated little ability to control volitionally their dating behavior. Similarly, obese individuals had only a modest capacity for volitionally controlling their eating and exercise behaviors. Conversely, using a broad sample of Notre Dame students, we found they had an enormous amount of volitional control over how much they eat. We compared the magnitude of this volitional control with a few environmental factors that previous research suggested were important, and found that on the average volitional control was *much, much more effective in controlling eating behavior than were the environmental factors!!* In fact, in a recent set of studies (Howard et al., 1988) we found that over 90 percent of the variance in a human action (drinking) can be unequivocally attributed to self-determination . . ."

"Is that a lot?"

"Is that a lot??? Oh! I see. Sarcasm again. *Eh bien*! I

guess I do get wrapped up in this stuff a bit. You know, I keep thinking of what physicists found when they investigated the nature of light to find out if light is basically a wave or a particle. It seems these investigations led to a rather unsatisfying but important conclusion: *If you ask it a wave question, it will give you a wave answer; ask it a particle question, and it will give you a particle answer.* It seems to me that in psychology we have been asking only mechanistic questions. We did so because those were the only types of questions we knew how to ask scientifically. But now we are also able to consider human action from the volitional/self-determining perspective. That's progress, and that's all you can ask from a discipline — that it try to improve.

Let me add that this research with personal agency is but one of hundreds of ways that psychology is improving as a scientific discipline. For example, since you know that theory development is the most important task of any science, you will be interested to know that a second generation of multivariate statistics (structural equation modeling techniques) have recently been developed that make the direct test of theory more likely to occur than had formerly been the case in psychological research. The field of psychoneuroimmunology is yet another area of promise. Recent developments demonstrate the important relationships among psychological states, subsequent levels of immune surveillance, and an individual's susceptibility to physical illness. Similarly, the insights of General Systems Theory have been brought to bear on a variety of human problems such as child abuse, alcoholism, and so forth. I have focused upon the recent developments that I know best, while a different psychologist might have attended to any of a number of equally promising scientific breakthroughs. But we don't have time to consider any others, do we?"

"No way!"

"This time you're right, Mike. Let me try to put what we've covered in a slightly different perspective by noting the following possibility. Almost five years ago, at graduation, I learned that Mahatma Ghandi felt there were seven sins in the world: wealth without work, pleasure without conscience, knowledge without character, commerce without morality, science without humanity, worship without sacrifice, and politics without principle. What did Ghandi mean by science without humanity? It appears the meaning might be very different for every science. For example, the possibility of the nuclear destruction of the human race represents a legacy that most physicists sorely regret. But psychology's ill-conceived bequest might be of a quite different sort. Our legacy could be an impoverished vision of humanity. By viewing humans from an unduly narrow perspective, we may perpetuate a paralyzing myopia that serves to diminish rather than expand humans' potential as individuals and as a species. Our challenge, then, would be to construct a science of humans built upon an image of humanity that reflects and reveres human nature in all its diversity, complexity, and subtlety — that is, an intellectual enterprise that truly deserves the designation of *A Human Science*. Well, there's the bell. Bet you thought it would never come."

"Professor, how much of this should be in our paper?"

"None of it! This was just an example of how to integrate some disparate ideas within psychology. This was easy. You people have got your work cut out for you. You've got to integrate all of the social sciences."

"Don't you think that assignment is a bit outrageous? After all, we're only sophomores."

"You're Notre Dame honors students, aren't you? Sit down and start playing with your ideas. You can sometimes amaze yourself when you work hard to polish up your thoughts. And then you will find out what you really do think. Or to paraphrase Shakespeare, 'What a piece of work is mind!' "

Chapter 13

Pumping Karma

So teach us to number our days, that we may apply our
hearts unto wisdom.
— Psalm 90

*Howard Sandler is one of the wisest people I know. We
were on our way to the airport —*
" . . .you just do it, Howard. It doesn't matter whether
you'll ever get repaid for it or not. It's the right thing to do, so you
do it. Make it a conscious effort. You see an opportunity to do
something — anything — good, kind, decent, or generous, and
you do it. Bang! Just like that you do it. Don't think about it. Act
now — think later. It becomes a habit — and a nice habit at that.
And the amazing thing is, if you're good to the world — it will be
good to you."
"Good karma!"
"What's karma? As old as I am , I don't know what karma
is."
**"Just that! It's exactly what you said. People
have a running bank account with the Universe. Do
something good or decent and you add to your store of
good karma. Do something mean and you add to your
bad karma. Keep piling up the bad karma — and you
come back in the next life as a cockroach!"**
"My God! We must have been terrible in our last lives —
we came back as psychologists!"
**"Right! And in Eastern thought, karma has
nothing to do with luck. Do good all your life and the
universe owes good back to you. Do bad and it'll come
back to haunt you."**
"While I don't believe in the reincarnation part, I think the
'running bank account with the Universe' part is a great strategy for
life. I believe that all those karma bank accounts will get settled-up
right here in this life in the long run."
**"I agree, George! Of course there is tremendous
evolutionary validity to philosophies that have thrived
for over five thousand years. Remember, this
Christianity thing is just a new kid on the block."**
"How old is *'Do unto others as you would have them do*

unto you?' "

"I don't know — but that's a handy way of knowing in which direction the good karma lies. If you'd like someone to treat you in a particular manner, chances are others will appreciate it if you'd treat them in the same way. Ditto if you wouldn't particularly like something else."

"Getting back to the point I was trying to make earlier, people should make a habit of working at building up their good karma. If you want a great body — you don't just sit around and wish you had a great body, you get on with the exercises — like pumping iron."

"So now you want me to think about 'Pumping Karma.' "

"Yes! Exactly! Face it, in all other skill domains of our lives we don't leave things to chance. We work on skills by practicing. We concentrate on developing the right set of habits. For example, if you want to be able to hit a particular shot in basketball, you practice it over and over again until it's virtually automatic. It almost becomes second nature to hit it. You ought to work at becoming good, decent, fair, reliable, objective, understanding, tolerant, and all those other 'good karma' ways of living. But the problem is that in the hustle-and-bustle of everyday life we tend to get caught up in what's going on. We react in a knee-jerk manner, rather than stopping to realize that we ought to be structuring each interaction in the hope that good karma will come out of it. You know what I mean — you just know nothing good will come from an interaction with a member of your faculty which begins with him or her shouting, 'I can't believe that you actually wrote that memo on who may use the xerox machine!'"

"No! I don't know that to be true. Most of the time good things come from interactions that start out badly. I turn them around by employing a very simple strategy. *I take everything as a compliment.* That's because almost everything that is said has some degree of ambiguity in it which you can use to your advantage. To that faculty member you mentioned I'd quickly say, 'Thank you! I agree that a policy statement on the use of the xerox machine was long overdue.' Depending on what the person had on his or her mind, the conversation will either be constructive or destructive in tone. But I guarantee that it is off to a far better start than if I'd reacted negatively to the opening line."

"And do you keep up that strategy throughout the conversation? I mean — every subsequent statement will also be somewhat ambiguous. Do you keep trying to take every additional remark in the conversation as a compliment?"

"Within reason, yes! Some statements are so negative that they couldn't possibly be construed as compliments, but you can always receive and interpret them in the best possible light. For example, if our irate faculty member says that the new xeroxing rules will slow down the work of his research assistants, I'd respond by highlighting the positive value that prompted his criticism. Depending upon the circumstance I might say something like, 'Yes, you are always doing your utmost to facilitate your research program, and it's precisely that single-minded dedication that makes you as successful at research as you are. Now let's see if there isn't some small adjustment to my new system that will meet the department's needs, and still won't slow your research program one iota. Got any suggestions?' It takes a bit of effort, creativity, and practice, but I've found that the quality of my interactions improves dramatically when I am consciously looking to see compliments in whatever others say to me."

"I don't think most people tend naturally to 'accentuate the positive' the way you do, Howard. Let's think about strategies to help folks to get better at dealing more positively with others, and in the process perhaps pump more good karma. And before you answer, I must tell you that I'm really skeptical because I've seen too many cases of people who try to use psychological techniques on other people, and it comes off as phoney. The people they 'try them out on' resent it because it feels really manipulative. I can easily imagine somebody trying to see everything as a compliment and doing it badly. People would react to it like 'What a bunch of happy-horseshit that joker is throwing at me. It stinks!'"

"Well, I'd certainly never want to be downwind of anybody acting like that. But I think you touch upon the right place to start — relationships should always be viewed as give-and-take propositions. One should always look at relationships from two separate perspectives — from your perspective *and* from the perspective of the other. A friend told me an interesting way to think about such interactions. It's called the **Win-Win box.** Suppose you think of our relationship, George.

George

Win   Lose

	Win	Lose
Win	A	B
Lose	C	D

Howard

I put your name at the top and mine on the side of the box. The left-hand column depicts situations wherein you win, and similarly, the top row is my win area. The right-hand column is your bad domain and the bottom row is my bad-land."

"Right, Howard, let's first label the boxes A through D. Now Box A represents the promised land. That's the goal for every relationship. In my opinion, both parties in any relationship should strive to have the relationship be in the A box. Some people have a bit of difficulty understanding how *both* members of a relationship can win. The problem stems from the fact that many games we designed and often play *require* that one team lose in order for the other to win. While this is a necessary requirement of most competitive games that we have created, it is not a necessary aspect of human relationships — even though some people see relationships as if there must be a winner and a loser. We see many people who view the world of human interactions in that way as clients in therapy. Psychologically speaking, it is a very destructive way to lead one's life, and often leads to social isolation and/or asymmetric, unsatisfying relationships.

"But let's look at a Win-Win relationship to see how one can analyze relationships into quadrants. I'll begin by analyzing our relationship, Howard. For my part, the 'costs' of our relationship are really minimal. Every once in a while I have to pick you up at the airport — which is really nothing. Sometimes, when you want to discuss some issue, it takes me away from other pressing work. But that's it! You are a wonderfully unobtrusive and self-sufficient house guest, and you have never imposed upon our friendship professionally. That's it. The 'costs' to me of our relationship are miniscule.

"Now for the benefits. First, you sharpen my thinking. In our discussions you point out every weak point in my thoughts — that's a big help. But you challenge and correct in a most helpful way. By that I mean that you try to help me toughen up the weaknesses. It is clear you probe with the goal of shoring up the weak spots. You want me to be as good a scholar as I can possibly become. Second, you make me a better department chair. You've been at this administration game longer than I, and the seasoning shows! I feel welcome in running any problem past you, and getting honest advice. Third, you fill in whenever our parenting system fails (e.g., babysit for a half hour; you care enough to correct our kids when we are not able to do so, etc.). Fourth, you have a great disposition and sense of humor. You're just fun to be around. I work too hard for my own good — but I don't work hard at all when you are around. That's good for me. Fifth, you know lots of things that I don't know — phenomenology, developmental psychology, Taoist philosophy, and so forth. I could go on with this list, but I think I've made my point. The benefits I receive from you so overwhelm the costs involved in our relationship that the costs could escalate enormously — like if something terrible happened to you and I jumped in to help — and I would still be firmly in the Win side (left column) in our relationship."

"From my perspective the costs are minimal as well. Aside from having to get up a little earlier than might otherwise be the case, and having to watch reruns of the Smurfs on the VCR, I have had a marvelous month visiting South Bend. You have gotten me back in the habit of writing again, which I greatly appreciate. You have made me walk two to five miles a day, which I greatly need. Our conversations during the walks are both enlightening and fun — I don't often get as sympathetic an audience for some of my strange ideas about the direction in which psychology is headed. Even the discussions about departmental matters have been very helpful to me. They have led me to rethink some of the things that I have been doing as department

chair, things that weren't working as well as they might have. In short, the benefits to me of our relationship also far outweigh the costs. I will return to Nashville a better (and healthier!) person."

"Phew! How did we ever get along, before we met? That little exercise should make two points clear: first, in relationships, somebody doesn't have to lose in order for someone else to win; and second, our lives are enriched by others, and thus we should seriously analyze and work toward making our relationships better. Have you been pumping good or bad karma so far today? What are you going to do about it?"

"George, let's look at other quadrants of your Win-Win box. Can you think of any relationship you now have which isn't Win-Win that we can analyze?'

"Unfortunately, I've got plenty of them. There's one I'd like to talk through, because I can't figure out if it's Win-Lose, Lose-Lose, or Lose-Win. There is a graduate student named Dan who is well on his way toward getting thrown out of the doctoral program for not making progress on his dissertation. So now let's replace 'Howard' with 'Dan' in the box. He's supposed to be working with me — but he shows up every six to eight months to get some stupid form signed — but he never mentions his dissertation. So here's the problem with the analysis of the relationship: since he makes no demands on me, it's hard to say that I'm losing. Given my track record as a research supervisor, no one will think he failed to succeed through any fault of mine. So it's hard to say I'm losing anything. But you can tell from the way I'm talking about it that I feel bad about the situation. Thus, I'd say that I'm probably on the losing side of the box (right side, either Box D or B). Now Dan is probably losing in the relationship also (bottom row, specifically Box D) because he isn't making any progress toward achieving his *stated* goal of getting a Ph.D. But I highlighted 'stated' because I'm just not sure that he still wants the degree anymore. He might have written off getting the degree long ago, and he might be effectively using this time to get ready for his next career move (top row, specifically Box B)."

"So you really don't know where you and he stand in your relationship. The next move is obvious; you should talk it over with Dan to find out where you stand with regard to one another. But George, you surely have figured that out. And yet, you haven't broached the topic with Dan. So more must be going on than you have let on."

"Yep! You are enormously insightful for a statistician. Oops, I hope I haven't damned you with faint praise? My problem in not talking to Dan falls under one of my rules of thumb (like your 'Take everything as a compliment'). My father told me this one: *'Never ask a question that you don't want to hear the answer to.'* My father never minded ending sentences with prepositions — he said people remembered them better that way."

"OK, let me guess what you're thinking. If you have a conversation where you bring up the fact that Dan's not making progress, and he says, 'You're right! Help me do a dissertation,' then you've got an undermotivated student, with program deadlines staring him in the face, on your hands. That's not a happy thought for someone as busy as you are right now."

"That's right, Howard. And if instead he says something like, 'I'm just writing computer software now so that I can be well on my way toward opening my own business when I drop out of the graduate program,' then I'm also in a jam. In that case, I would have some ethical responsibility to force his hand, since he is tying up University resources and has no intention of using them properly. So I'm having a hard time imagining a happy ending to this scenario. Thus, since the ball is now in his court, I'm not taking any action at this point in time. If I could imagine a possible happy outcome, I would act to bring it about."

"OK. I can see why your relationship with Dan isn't Win-Win right now. My problem involves a few people I must work with now who are acting really immaturely and it's driving me crazy. They are adults — faculty members — and they ought to think and act more maturely. If I think of it in Win-Win terms, will it help me to feel better about my job?"

"I think so. Let's think it through. I assume that you are successfully facilitating this person's work, and rather than being appreciative of your efforts, the person just makes your life miserable."

"Exactly. He acts like the entire world should be anxiously waiting to be of service to him and his needs. His attitude is really quite immature and frustrating. He should be grateful for all the University has done for him — but instead his needs seem insatiable. So, I guess it is probably a Win (for him) — Lose (for me) situation."

"The first step I'd recommend, Howard, is that you simply

lay out the situation to him exactly the way you just did for me. Suppose he objects. Howard, you and I know that you go the extra mile for everyone. So I'd just say that if he will not be cooperative, you'll be forced to give him his fair share of departmental resources — no more, no less. Further, you will be forced (by him) to live up to the letter of the law of your job description — no more, no less. He makes you take this step because the present arrangement makes you feel ripped-off — so now you need to take measures to protect your feelings. How would he react to that?"

"Well, first we'd have to pick him up off the floor and revive him. He would starve if he only got his fair share."

"Precisely! Howard, you've been carrying this joker for too long already — and feeling miserable in the process. Either he takes the responsibility for doing whatever is necessary to move you from Win-Lose to Win-Win, or the relationship becomes purely formal and legalistic. That's not too much to ask of an adult — is it? Even if he forces you to the formal relationship, you'd probably feel fine about that. Let me make one other point. It wasn't a really risky guess on my part to suggest that he was already getting more than his share of the resources. In most organizations it is 'the squeaky wheel that gets the grease.' This guy has learned over the years that 'squeaking' gets results. You've got to send the message to your folks that squeaking gets you pissed — and gets them in trouble."

"I do! I even got a memo out on that. It's the people who work hard and are the good departmental citizens who get special treatment. The thing that makes it tough with the guy we're discussing is that he is a good scholar and teacher. If he were unproductive, I would have held his feet to the fire long ago. But it would be a real loss to the University if this guy took a job somewhere else. That's why I put up with a bit more crap than I would have for normal faculty members."

"Yep! That's going to make it a bit more difficult for you to negotiate a Win-Win situation with this guy. Both you and he know that he has a power base due to his competence. Fortunately, you are as competent as he; you have position power since you are the department chair; and, most important, you are *right*. He's needlessly making your life miserable. He should be expected to make reasonable efforts to make your job more bearable.

But more needs to be said about the role of power in these attempts to bring about Win-Win relationships. As a general rule of thumb, if you are in a position of superior power you need not seriously fear opening up a discussion aimed at reaching a fair (i.e., a solution both would endorse if there were no power differential) settlement. Since you do have the power — you could enforce an unfair solution. But that would be a mistake, from the good karma perspective. Thus, you must be *very* sensitive to the 'Do unto others as you would have them do unto you' perspective. Make sure that you haven't forced the other person into a bad deal that they are agreeing to *only* because you hold the power. After a good deal (Win-Win) has been struck, I take a moment to see if I can think of any 'pot-sweeteners.' Those are little 'add-ons' that I can throw in to make it a better deal for the other person. I only suggest 'add-ons' that I feel good about — that is, things I don't mind doing for the other person that I know they will appreciate.

If you are in a Win-Lose situation where you are losing and the other person is in the position of power — proceed with great caution. The best way to broach the issue is under the cover of pursuing ways in which the relationship could become more lucrative for the person in power (e.g., "Howard, I might have the time to try for an NSF grant if I just didn't have so many teaching duties next semester"). Make that proposal if you want to reduce your teaching load — especially if you plan to try for the grant anyhow."

"George, I tell my faculty that work counts — it counts for *a lot*! As long as that faculty member is willing to do an honest day's work, I'm convinced we can strike a Win-Win arrangement."

"There's no doubt in my mind that you're absolutely right on that score, Howard. In fact, you are precisely the type of boss for whom each of us would love to work. But that brings us to the most difficult — but by far the most important — concept of this entire conversation. It is absolutely essential that you correctly assess the character of the person with whom you are dealing. There are good people out there — and there are some mean, sick, bad dudes out there. You have to protect yourself from getting used by such individuals. Nothing can sour someone on people as fast as a series of relationships with mean, self-centered, egotistical, and selfish sleazeballs. Hope I didn't blow you away with all that psychological jargon. Wait a minute. I'm getting down-and-dirty a bit too fast. This crucial issue of assessment should be approached a bit more analytically."

"Aw nuts! I want to hear more about the 'egotistical sleazeballs!' Gimme names."

"Be serious! Howard, one of the reasons I like you so much is because of your attitude toward your wife and daughter. Soon after we met, you began telling stories about them, and gradually your relationships with them began to become apparent. Your love, support, and consideration for them tells us a lot about you — and how you view others in your life. Second, we have some mutual friends who consistently speak very highly of you. Finally, our early interactions had a good feel to them. I can't be specific as to what it was exactly, but my clinical intuition told me you were a good person — one who could be trusted. I put a lot of faith in my initial impressions of people. Fortunately, trusting my intuition almost invariably proves to be a good *modus operandi* for me.

I can remember only two instances where my gut reaction was completely wrong. Once I got taken for a ride by a really skilled sociopath for whom I worked. It took me months to realize that he was only using me — and everyone else for that matter. Boy that bugger was a dangerous person. He was unbelievably skilled at deceit — and deception. My other poor first assessment was a woman whom I disliked a lot when I first met her. Turns out she is a wonderful person. I still haven't figured out why I misread her so badly.

Assessment is critical in pumping good karma because you need to protect your attitude toward others. Some people are good karma black holes. If you get taken advantage of often enough, you soon sour on people in general, and gradually you lose your will to trust others. That can lead to a death spiral of suspicion-isolation-depression that, in extreme cases, can completely destroy one's support system. Surround yourself with good people, and you'll become a much better person. Did you know that a key therapeutic strategy for depression involves helping the client just to spend more time with people he or she likes and at the same time trying to minimize the amount of time he or she spends with people who 'bum them out?' "

"Yes, I heard about that approach. Tell depressed clients to 'cheer up' or 'become less depressed,' and they can't do anything with that advice. In fact, that's why they came to therapy in the first place — they can't control their attitude as well as one would normally be able to do. But often they can follow their therapist's suggestion that they spend more time with Carol and Bob (who are people they enjoy) and spend less time with Mary and Mr. Jones (people who bring them down). They typically don't see how this will 'cure their depression,' but when they do it, they almost always feel a bit better. Obviously, more is usually required than simply improving one's support system, but these improvements are important actions, and do help one's attitude immensely."

"So there might be real validity to the old saying 'Show me your friends and I'll tell you what kind of person you are.' It's good advice actively to seek out warm, wholesome, pleasant people because of the impact they will have on your attitude — and your life overall. So pick out the people that your intuition tells you will return your good will, and actively work at 'pumping good karma.' I think your life will be richer for having done so."

"Being nice to people is important to me, George, but reminding myself that I could be wrong in my first impressions is usually an important step toward a better understanding of other people."

"How so? Besides, isn't it hard on your self-esteem to be constantly reminding yourself of your own fallibility?"

"My self-esteem seems to be holding up pretty well so far."

"That's for sure!"

"Let's get back to your questions. Relying on my first impressions of someone can lead to a self-fulfilling prediction about my future relationship with him or her. If I believe that I am going to like someone and then follow up that belief with friendly behavior, then that person may be more inclined to act in a friendly manner toward me. Of course, if I decide that I am likely not to become friends with someone, then I may act in ways that do not promote good feelings in the other person. In either case, the other person is likely to respond in kind to my actions. Understanding that I could be wrong in my first impressions means that I understand that the other person may have just had a bad day, or may be shy, or may be wondering why I am staring at him or her. Giving the person a chance by my showing interest may be just the thing to get a positive interaction going.

I don't think that I ever told you how I met my wife. It's a strange story, but illustrates the point. I was a senior in college at Hopkins and 'in between' relationships. One Friday evening during the spring semester, a friend of mine and I decided to drive down to the University of Maryland to see if we could find some of our friends who were in school there. While my friend was off looking for someone, I went over to sorority row to find my cousin, Diane, and say hello to her. It turned out that all of the sororities were holding 'mixers' on this particular Friday night. As I entered the foyer of the sorority house I noticed an attractive, well-dressed young woman standing by herself. I assumed that she was some sort of official 'greeter' for the sorority, so I smiled and greeted her. She smiled and greeted me right back. When I asked her if she knew my cousin, Diane, she seemed very confused. First, she didn't know how it was possible that I knew her name, which was also Diane, and, second, she didn't know my cousin. I found all of this to be quite unusual. I couldn't imagine that she didn't know my cousin since they were 'obviously' in the same sorority.

Well, what was obvious to me was far from obvious to anyone else. Diane, my future wife, was not a 'greeter' for the sorority. She went to another college that was a few hundred miles away and was using her spring break to visit a (male) cousin. She had been left at the sorority house by her cousin while he went to bring back her blind date for the next night and introduce them to each other. Her cousin was taking longer than promised, and Diane, feeling as though she were intruding because she really didn't know anyone in the sorority, had decided to wait in the foyer. Her first reaction to my 'knowing' her name was that her cousin had put me up to this and that I was her blind date. By the time we had straightened out our common confusion we were laughing and having a good time. Her cousin and her blind date eventually showed up, but Diane and I were practically engaged by then."

"That's quite a story. Both you and Diane were wrong in you first impressions of each other. You thought that she was a 'greeter' so you greeted her, and she thought that you were her blind date, so she was being friendly. Getting off to a good start worked out pretty well, didn't it?"

"I better say 'yes' or else we will be talking about my 'former wife.' The interesting part to me is the fact that Diane is actually fairly shy, so that she might not have greeted me if I hadn't seen her as a greeter. My prediction about her behavior led to her acting as I had predicted rather than to how she might ordinarily have acted. Similarly, her having seen me as someone with whom she was going to have to spend an evening made my friendly behavior seem appropriate rather than 'forward.'"

"I am not going to let you off of the hook about the question of self-esteem. How do you maintain a good self-image while thinking that you could be wrong?"

"Actually, it seems to take the pressure off because I no longer have to be right every time. Every encounter is an adventure — I never know in advance how they will turn out. I always learn something from each person that I meet. The more I learn, the more I know, so my self-esteem goes up. It's all very logical!"

"Howard, you seem to have a lot of respect for other people. It's not often that you find that quality in psychologists."

"Thank you, George. It's all a part of my underlying belief that, if I try hard enough, I can learn something from almost anyone. The hard part is to make sure that I learn the right thing from them."

"Good point! You certainly wouldn't want to learn table manners from my children. What could you learn from them?"

"Well, I could learn something about how young children react to me, and about what I can do to make my interactions with them more enjoyable for all of us. Perhaps I could learn something about myself from my reactions to their behavior. I could even learn something from you and Nancy about dealing with small, tired people. There are lots of opportunities for me to learn something by being around your children."

"Then you could learn something different on each occasion?"

"Exactly! But I can't always have in mind a specific thing that I wish to learn. Sometimes I have to work hard just to figure out what I can learn from a situation. Sometimes I am too tired (or too lazy) to learn something — then it's my loss. Timing is everything. When I first started playing bridge, for example, I was able to learn quite a bit about the basics from some people who weren't very good players. Later on, I learned a lot about what not to do by watching the mistakes that those same players made. Although they hadn't changed at all, I was still able to learn new things from them."

"Can you learn anything when you are teaching?"

"Of course you can. Two years ago, my daughter, Robin, asked me to teach her how to play tennis so that she could go out and play with her friends. I found that it was easier for me to control where the ball landed when I hit a backhand shot, so I spent most of the summer hitting backhands to her. After a few weeks of playing, Robin was concerned that I might not be enjoying myself playing tennis with her, and that I might rather be playing with someone who played better than she did. I told her that I was getting a lot of practice with my backhand, and that I didn't know anyone else who would be so tolerant of my hitting only backhand shots. The 'net' results were that my daughter learned to play tennis, my backhand improved dramatically, and my daughter and I found a new way to enjoy each other's company.

Let me switch to a more serious example: making friends. Although my daughter has made many friends over the years, it took a lot of work on her part, and often a lot of pain. I remember one girl with whom she was friends — Denise (I think it was). At any rate, she and my daughter had been friends for a few years when an incident occurred where my daughter felt that Denise had let her down badly. I didn't think that the incident was as serious as my daughter was treating it, but I couldn't convince her to lower her expectations of how a 'true friend' would have acted in the situation. Needless to say, the friendship ended abruptly. What do you think that my daughter learned from this incident?"

"I hope that it wasn't something like 'having friends is no good because they'll only let you down.' "

"Fortunately not. It was more like 'friendship isn't all or none, it comes in degrees.' It took a while for her to understand that it is better to have realistic expectations for your friends. It was probably impossible, for example, that Denise could have continued to live up to my daughter's expectations. Later on, though, another of my daughter's friends, Kate, went through a period of unreliability as a friend."

"What happened this time? Another friendship shot down in flames?"

"No, not this time. This time Robin was able to lower her expectations for Kate while still enjoying her company. She and Kate have been able to maintain their friendship despite some rocky periods."

"One thing bothers me about these stories — I think that friendships take a lot of work. I hope that your daughter also learned that somewhere along the line."

"She did, but it was a painful struggle. Her very best friend is a girl named Julie, and Julie has had some very difficult periods in her own life. During those periods, she has had a hard time being a good friend, yet at the same time has been very much in need of friendship. Robin has always been there for Julie, even at times when it was difficult for her to do so. It finally got to the point where Robin felt that the friendship was becoming a one-way street — after all, she had needs, too. Just when I thought that the friendship was about to collapse, however, Julie came through in an important way for Robin. It turned out that she had learned a lot about being a friend as well. Even though in some ways Robin and Julie have outgrown their friendship with one another, there will always be warm feelings between them. The friendship won't remain the same as they go off to college and out into the world, but at least they can feel good about having *grown* apart, rather than having fallen apart. They both learned that friendship takes work, and they will both have better relationships with others for having learned it."

"Well, here we are at the airport. I'm sorry your flight goes through Chicago — O'Hare can be a mad house. Besides, those clouds are beginning to look ominous.

This has been a fascinating conversation — but I'm at a loss as to how to summarize it so that I won't forget it. Got a way of summarizing it?"

"Sure! Do good! In fact, work hard at doing good for others. Do it in the way that feels natural and right for you. Look for the best in others as best you can — like taking everything as a compliment. And surround yourself with good, wholesome, loving people.

I've got to run! Say goodbye to Nancy, John, and Greg."

"Sure! Give my love to Diane and Robin — and good luck with O'Hare."

Chapter 14

Imagine

Life's like a movie,
Write your own ending.
Keep believing, keep pretending.
We've done just what we set out to do.
As do the lovers, the dreamers, and you.

—Kermit the Frog, *The Muppet Movie*

Tying Down Some Loose Ends

These last few chapters have been pretty wild! I mean, Doc, Howard, and I threw a little bit of everything at you. Part of it was straightforward, sober scholarship. For example, the exercise study recognizes the force of the *psychologist's fallacy* (see Lamiel, 1987) and shows how the intensive study of the individual can avoid that problem. But our desire for lawlike relationships that hold at the group level can also be satisfied by the aggregation of findings from individuals. The key here is to analyze first (at the level of the individual) and then aggregate. (*Do not* aggregate and then analyze, cf. Valsiner, 1986) So that little study points toward one solution to the *psychologist's fallacy* problem. But it also demonstrates how a final cause factor — namely, self-determination — can be studied rigorously. That's very valuable knowledge to obtain. It allows us to begin to study the implications of the model of humans proposed in Chapter 12. Finally, the last five chapters show important connections between the scientific study of self-determination and the clinical practice of psychotherapy. I hope such linkages will begin to heal some of the wounds created by the scientist-practitioner schism. All of this represents serious, sober scholarship — I am convinced I could defend all of the above claims easily.

But the last five chapters also dealt with issues in philosophy of science, psychology and religion, and wisdom for living. Some of those ideas were rather speculative. While I believe all of what was said to be true, I would have a devil of a time defending some of it. But that is the essence of the scientific imagination. Scientists first *hope* that their vision of the nature of the phenomenon (like, for psychologists, human beings) is true. For example, Skinner hopes humans are reinforcement seekers; Maslow hopes people are self-actualizers; I hope persons are storytellers and self-determining; Freud hopes humans are unconsciously motivated; Rhyne hopes people possess psychic powers; James hopes human beings have spiritual capacities; and so forth. It is only one's hope that leads one to the discovery of something. Or as Heraclitus put it, unless you hope, you will not find the unhoped for. And the human imagination plays an enormous role in the creation of human hope.

But for the scientific psychologist an imagined and hoped-for human capacity is but the first step. The next step is to imagine how such a human capacity (if it did exist) could be demonstrated in an experiment. As suggested earlier, the empirical demonstration is to the scientist what paint is to the artist; clay is to the sculptor; stories are to the novelist; and arguments are to the philosopher. There are both beautiful and flawed works of art; both insightful and mundane stories; both reasonable and flawed arguments; and, finally, both compelling and uninteresting scientific studies. What makes a particular psychological study compelling? An experiment is enlightening when: 1) it succeeds in demonstrating human powers or capacities that had heretofore been considered impossible of humans; or 2) it demonstrates a particular power or capacity and is methodologically able to eliminate competing explanations of the phenomenon quite effectively. But it requires tremendous creativity and insight to create an experiment whose findings are dramatic and/or logically compelling. Creative scientists conduct versions of their experiments in their minds thousands of times before they settle upon the precise set of experimental procedures they will employ to obtain their data.

Every secret of a writer's soul, every experience of his life,
every quality of his mind is written large in his works.
— Virginia Woolf

Reframing the Past Within an Imagined Future

There is no history — only biography.
— Ralph Waldo Emerson

While our lifestories help us to make sense of the past,

their most important function is to help us to anticipate (and create) the future. It is in this sense that I agree with Smith and Vetter's (1982) claim that, "It is not the past or present but the *future* which determines behavior. . ." (p. 239). Recall the talk I gave at an APA convention (in Chapter 7) about my professional aims. Vince said, ". . . a course in assessment really isn't important to the person who is going to make research in humanistic psychology respectable!" While I doubted his sanity at the time, a seed had been planted. By 1985 I was marveling at Vince's prescience: "About a dozen years ago, a good friend dangled a fat, juicy worm in front of a frisky, young Sucker, and urged him to swim with it as far as he could. Vince asked me to be part of a story. And frankly, it's still the nicest story anyone has ever invited me to take part in." But the best was (and hopefully *still is*) yet to come!

Recall Professor Santa Barbara's claim that demonstrating that a person could follow a pattern of behavior, like the pattern the moon was asked to follow, would not convince psychologists that the behavior was self-determined. All other possible explanations for the person's behavior would have to be eliminated before scientific psychologists would cry *credo*. Happily, Howard and Conway (1986) presented the first of several demonstrations that make precisely this point. Self-determination accounts for huge amounts of variance in human behavior, even when all other possible causes of that action are methodologically eliminated as reasonable explanations. But Santa Barbara longed for even stronger empirical demonstrations of agency:

> . . . I would want to see some action that reeks of intelligence before I would feel comfortable that the demonstration undeniably was the work of an intelligent agent. For example, if the moon could turn on and off whether or not it reflected the sun's light to us, I would love to see the moon flash on and off a message in morse code — how about 'Moon Person on Board.' That would sure knock my socks off! . . . Professor Big Ten was obviously tickled with the points being made because he roared with laughter at the thought of the moon writing a letter across the sky to astronomers everywhere.

I can guarantee that Howard, Curtin, and Johnson (1988) were as tickled as Professor Big Ten to demonstrate that human beings were enormously accurate in flashing messages (e.g., Free Will; Love; Mother) in morse code to psychologists everywhere.

These research subjects communicated by the precise patterning of various behaviors (e.g., alcohol consumption, milk consumption) in several studies. Further, the research demonstrated that peoples' ability to self-determine was a function of the *meaningfulness* of the acts requested of them, *ceteris paribus* (all other factors being equal [i.e., controlled methodologically]).

So humans are active agents, and an action's meaningfulness to the agent is an important aspect of the person's ability to fine tune his or her control over the behavior of interest. Well, how do humans infuse their lives with meaning? This book suggests that people tell themselves stories that can infuse certain parts of their lives and actions with great meaning, and deemphasize other aspects. But had any of them chosen to tell himself or herself a somewhat different story, the resulting pattern of more-meaningful and less-meaningful aspects of his or her life would have been quite different. And the best part of this story of a human science is still to come. I am now imagining how we'll fit together the next few pieces in this puzzle of the role of self-determination in the wellsprings of human action. But, alas, the empirical demonstrations have not yet been conducted and interpreted. So I guess you'll have to wait a while for the next installment. But as I now close my eyes, I can imagine the members of our research group sitting around a table, composing the report of those studies. You'll get to read them someday soon — for it's that vision which will serve to bring about that imagined future — in some psychology journal ("Good Lord willing, and the creek don't rise!" — Pauline Wright).

A Final Look at Some Themes

Knowledge and Wisdom

> *I have gradually come to understand what every great philosophy . . . has been: the confession of its author and a kind of involuntary, unconscious memoir.*
> — Friedrich Nietzsche

The relationship between wisdom and knowledge is currently quite problematic throughout the social sciences and, indeed, throughout society. Science is increasingly seen as an all-purpose approach for obtaining veridical knowledge. Our best sources of wisdom have always been the tacit (or commonsense) knowledge each of us extracts from our interactions with the world and other people throughout life; enduring social and cultural institutions like schools, political movements, religions, the family, and so forth; and scholarship in the fine arts and humanities. But a problem arises when one realizes that the knowledge obtained by scientific psychology and the wisdom gleaned from life, society, and humanistic scholarship are both concerned with the same subject matter — namely, human beings. While these similar interests might suggest that insights from both perspectives could be compatible, in practice cross-fertilization and interaction are rather limited. Some true synthesis, that lessened the current tensions between knowledge and wisdom, would be most welcome.

Imagine a model of human action, like that depicted in Figure 7 of Chapter 12, where the *self* is seen as the organizing entity (or serving the executive function) in a person's life. Such a model is *finally* eminently scientific and testable. In time we will have ample empirical evidence to suggest the degree to which humans exert causal force in self-determining their actions. And, if self-determination proves to be an important element in the genesis of human action, the next question becomes obvious. How is such agentic control achieved?

This book contends that at its core, the self is a storytelling entity [See also chapter 14 of Howard (1986a) entitled "The Self as a Center of Narrative Gravity"]. Some stories are more hopeful than others, and allow the storyteller greater power for self-determination in his or her life than do other types of stories. But, of course, there are limits imposed by our material nature, our environment, our upbringing, our cultural inheritance, and so forth that set upper bounds upon our ability to self-determine in any domain. We're now finally ready for this book's most speculative move. *Wisdom in human life is a function of the character of (or the meaning embedded within) the stories we are choosing to tell ourselves about our lives.* There is potentially an infinite set of stories one could tell about a person's life — all of which are completely consistent with the facts of the life. Similarly, there are innumerable possible true stories of science. I simply told you *A Story of George* and *A Story of Science*. The meaning of (and wisdom contained within) my life and the history of science would have been quite different, had I chosen to tell different stories about these historical realities.

Admittedly, the picture is still rather mirky in my own mind — but I think I see the glimmerings of an understanding of human beings that is an integration of wisdom and knowledge. It's still a longshot that this mirky vision will someday be clear and compelling to more psychologists than "just me and a few good friends." But I do know that the vision won't mature and improve unless my friends and I imagine and hope for its maturity. I have thirty years until mandatory retirement. If I'm given the gift of that much time, with diligence, I should be able to finish Vince's story.

The Future of the Scientist-Practitioner Schism

Time wounds all heels.
— Goodman Ace

Numerous writers (e.g., Cohen, 1977; Goldman, 1976; Gelso, 1979) have noted the crippling effects of this contemporary problem. Helpful, scholarly interactions between scientific psychologists and practitioners are few and far between, and even our main professional organization — the American Psychological Association — is badly torn along scientist-practitioner lines. But I see a good deal of hope for a resolution in the not too distant future (Boy, that's a stunner! Me? Optimistic?).

Imagine practitioners conducting therapy like Doc did in Chapter 9. That represents good science (I would maintain), and probably would also be decent therapy. I believe the research methodologies employed twenty years from now will bear a striking resemblance to the clinical practices of today, and will be very dissimilar to the research methodologies employed in the research literature today. (See Howard 1985c, 1986b for fuller justification and elaboration of that point.) I also predict that we will see a good deal more analysis of the *meaning* of what clients think and say. Such studies will learn much from phenomenological psychology, hermeneutics, ethnomethodology, psychobiography, and literary criticism. Stated slightly differently, I am convinced that there will be a revolution in psychological research when we finally realize that *meaning-creation through storytelling represents the mind's equivalent of the body's immune system.*

Psychology and Religion

An artist, great or small, works for the salvation of his own soul above all other things.
— J. Middleton Murry

I believe that we have already entered a new age of development in the psychology of religion. The work shortly to come in this important domain will (please, God) not only represent good scholarship but it also will generate excitement in professionals such as theologians, philosophers, psychologists and others, within relevant disciplines. I already see movement toward potential joint topics from philosophers (e.g., MacIntyre, 1981; Evans, 1988); psychologists (e.g., Myers, 1978; Van Leeuwen, 1985, 1988); and theologians (Dunne, 1988; Buber, 1975). But as with all cross-disciplinary efforts, progress will probably be slow.

It's easy for me to imagine fruitful interaction and useful cross-fertilization among philosophers, theologians, and psychologists. But perhaps that is because the philosophers and theologians with whom I've chosen to interact are all such insightful, open-minded, interesting, and helpful people. And, of course, we psychologists are the very soul of insight and open-mindedness. How could such an alliance possibly fail?

You see things; and you say, "Why?"
But I dream things that never were;
and I say "Why not?"
— George Bernard Shaw

If you are interested in an absolutely stunning integration of religious belief with contemporary psychology, I urge you to read Bill Miller's (1985) brilliant *Living As If*.

> Living as if is a process of becoming . . . It is a
> peculiar combination of recognizing the gap between
> present reality and what one wants to become, of
> hoping for that change, and of becoming a new
> being. It is the twilight zone of change. Living as if
> does not deny present reality; it changes that reality.

It is a dazzling example of the best that religion and psychology has to offer. My prediction is that in the future such happy cross-fertilization will become the norm — not the exception.

Life, Family, Friendship, and Love

I, too, have tried in my time to be a philosopher; but I don't know
how, cheerfulness was always breaking in.
— Oliver Edwards

I have no wisdom to offer on these important topics. But I think Amanda McBroom offers enormous insight in my favorite song "The Rose." But the experience of a song is impoverished if it is reduced to words and presented as text. This might be an appropriate time to apologize for all of the times in this book that I tried to convey a rich human experience in mere words. I'm sorry that you only got the impoverished experience of the text. And so I'll end this book with a request. If you know "The Rose" please perform the work of art as it was intended. Don't just read it. Do me the kindness of singing the song. After all, we are not like the moon — life is *lived in the first person;* to be experienced, not merely contemplated. So go for it!

Some say love it is a river that drowns the tender reed,
Some say love it is a razor that leaves your soul to bleed.
Some say love it is a hunger, an endless aching need,
I say love it is a flower and you its only seed.

It's the heart afraid of breaking that never learns to dance,
It's the dream afraid of waking that never takes the chance.
It's the one who won't be taken who cannot seem to give,
And the soul afraid of dying that never learns to live.

When the night has been too lonely and the road has been too long,
And you think that love is only for the lucky and the strong.
Just remember in the winter far beneath the bitter snows,
Lies the seed that with the sun's love in the Spring becomes the rose.

—Amanda McBroom, *The Rose*

References

Adler, M. J. (1958, 1961). The idea of freedom. Garden City, N.Y.: Doubleday. Two volumes.

Bandura, A. (1977). Self-efficacy: Toward unifying theory of behavioral change. Psychological Review, 84, 191-215.

Bandura, A. (1982). The psychology of chance encounters and life paths. American Psychologist, 37, 747-755.

Bandura, A. (1986). Social foundations of thought and action: A social cognitive theory. Englewood Cliffs: Prentice-Hall.

Barlow, D. H., Hayes, S. C., & Nelson, R. O. (1984). The scientist practitioner: Research and accountability in clinical and educational settings. Elmsford, N.Y.: Pergamon.

Bateson, G. (1979). Mind and nature: A necessary unity. New York: Dutton

Bellah, R. N. et al. (1985). Habits of the heart. Berkeley: University of California Press.

Berger, P. L. (1963). Invitation to sociology: A humanistic perspective. New York: Doubleday & Co.

Bronowski, J. (1973). The ascent of man. Boston: Little-Brown.

Buber, M. (1958). I and thou. New York: Scribner.

Campbell, D. T. (1975). On the conflicts between biological and social evolution and between psychology and moral tradition. American Psychologist, 30, 1103-1126.

Cohen, J. (1977). Statistical power analysis in the behavioral sciences. New York: Academic Press.

Cohen, L. H. (1977). The research readership and information source reliance of clinical psychologists. Professional Psychology, 10, 780-785.

Cook, T. D. (1985). Postpositivist critical multiplism. In R. L. Shotland & M. M. Mark (Eds.) Social science and social policy. Beverly Hills: Sage.

Cook, T. D., & Campbell, D. T. (1979). Quasi-experimentation: Design and analysis issues for field settings. Chicago: Rand McNally.

Cooper, K. H. (1970). The new aerobics. New York: Evans.

de Charms, R. (1968). Personal causation. New York: Academic Press.

Deci, E. L. (1980). Self-determination. Lexington, Mass.: Lexington Books.

Evans, C. S. (1988). Psychology as a human science: Prospects for a Christian approach. (in preparation).

Ferre, F. (1973). Self-determinism. American Philosophical Quarterly, 10, 165-176.

Ford, D. H. (1987). Humans as self-constructing living systems: A developmental perspective on personality and behavior. Hillsdale, N.J.: Erlbaum.

Frank, J. D. (1961). Persuasion and healing. Baltimore: Johns Hopkins.

Freud, S. (1927). The future of an illusion. New York: Liveright, 1949.

Freud, S. (1965). The psychopathology of everyday life. New York: Norton.

Gabbard, C. E., Howard, G. S., & Dunfee, E. J. (1986). Reliability, sensitivity to measuring change, and construct validity of a measure of counselor adaptability. Journal of Counseling Psychology, 33, 377-386.

Gelso, C. J. (1979). Research in counseling: Methodological and professional issues. The Counseling Psychologist, 8, 7-35.

Gelso, C. J. (1985). Rigor, relevance, and counseling research: On the need to maintain our course between Scylla and Charybdis. Journal of Counseling and Development, 63, 551-553.

Gelso, C. J. & Carter, J. A. (1985). The relationship in counseling and psychotherapy: Components, consequences, and theoretical antecedents. The Counseling Psychologist, 13, 155-243.

Gergen, K. J. (1982). Toward transformation in social knowledge. New York: Springer-Verlag.

Gergen, K. J., & Gergen, M. M. (1986). Narrative and the self as relationship. In L. Berkowitz (Ed.), Advances in experimental social psychology. New York: Academic Press.

Goldman, L. (1976). A revolution in counseling research. Journal of Counseling Psychology, 23, 543-552.

Harré, R. (1985). Personal being. Cambridge, Mass.: Harvard University Press.

Hersey, P. & Blanchard, K. H. (1977). Management of organizational behavior: Utilizing human resources (3rd ed.). Englewood Cliffs, N.J.: Prentice-Hall.

Howard, G. S. (1985a). Basic research methods the social sciences. Glenview, Ill.: Scott Foresman.

Howard, G. S. (1985b). The role of values in the science of psychology. American Psychologist, 40, 255-265.

Howard, G. S. (1985c). Can research in the human sciences become more relevant to practice? Journal of Counseling and Development, 63, 539-544.

Howard, G. S. (1986a). Dare we develop a human science? Notre Dame, Ind.: Academic Publications.

Howard, G. S. (1986b). The scientist-practitioner model in counseling psychology: Toward a deeper integration of theory, research, and practice. The Counseling Psychologist, 14, 61-105.

Howard, G. S. (1987). The person in research. Person-Centered Review, 2, 50-62.

Howard, G. S. (1988). Can science provide evidence of human freedom? Nature (in press).

Howard, G. S. & Conway, C. G. (1986). Can there be an empirical science of volitional action? American Psychologist, 41, 1241-1251.

Howard, G. S., Curtin, T. D., & Johnson, A. J. (1988). The hardening of a 'soft' science. Invited address: Mathematical and Statistical Models of Behavior Track, Science Weekend, APA Convention, Atlanta.

Howard, G. S., Di Gangi, M., & Johnson, A. J. (1988). Life, science, and the role of therapy in the pursuit of happiness. Professional Psychology: Research and Practice, 19, 191-198.

Howard, G. S., Nance, D. W. & Myers, P. (1986). Adaptive counseling and therapy: An integrative, eclectic model. The Counseling Psychologist, 14, 363-442.

Howard, G. S., Nance, D. W. & Myers, P. (1987). Adaptive counseling and therapy: A systematic approach for selecting effective treatments. San Francisco: Jossey-Bass.

Howard G. S., Youngs, W. H., & Siatczynski, A. M. (1988). Reforming methodology in psychological research. Journal of Mind and Behavior.

Immergluck, L. (1964). Determinism-freedom in contemporary psychology: An ancient problem revisited. American Psychologist, 19, 270-281.

James, W. (1958). The varieties of religious experience. New York: The New American Library.

Kimble, G. A. (1984). Psychology's two cultures. American Psychologist, 39, 833-839.

Koch, S., & Leary, D. E. (Eds.) (1985). A century of

psychology as science. New York: McGraw-Hill.

Kuhn, T. (1977). The essential tension. Chicago: University of Chicago Press.

Lamiel, J. T. (1987). The psychology of personality: An epistemological inquiry. New York: Columbia University Press.

Larsen, J., & Nichols, D. (1972). If nobody knows you've done it, have you? Evaluation, 1, 39-44.

Lazarick, D. L., Fishbein, S. S., Loiello, M. J., & Howard, G. S. (1988). Practical investigations of volition. Journal of Counseling Psychology, 35, 15-26.

Lazarus, A. A. (1976). Multimodal behavior therapy. New York: Springer.

Lazarus, A. A. (1985). Casebook of multimodal therapy. New York: Guilford.

Leary, D. E. (1987). Telling likely stories: The rhetoric of the new psychology, 1880-1920. Journal of the History of the Behavioral Sciences, 23, 315-331.

Leftcourt, H. M. (1973). The function of the illusions of control and freedom. American Psychologist, 28, 417-425.

Loevinger, J. (1987). Paradigms of Personality. New York: W. H. Freeman.

MacIntyre, A. (1981). After virtue. Notre Dame, IN: University of Notre Dame Press.

Marx, K. (1843). In the "Introduction" of the Critique of Hegel's philosophy of right. In the 1843 German-French Yearbook (magazine).

McMullin, E. (1983). Values in science. In P. D. Asquith & T. Nickles (Eds.), Proceedings of the 1982 Philosophy of Science Association (Vol. 2, pp. 3-23). East Lansing, Mich.: Philosophy of Science Association.

McMullin, E. (1984). The goals of natural science. Proceedings and Addresses of the American Philosophical Association, 58, 37-64.

McMullin, E. (1985). Evolution and creation. Notre Dame, Ind.: University of Notre Dame Press.

Milgram, S. (1974). Obedience to authority. New York: Harper & Row.

Miller, W. R. (1985). Living as if: How positive faith can change your life. Philadelphia: Westminster Press.

Mischel, W. & Grusec, J. (1967). Waiting for rewards and punishments: Effects of time and probability of choice. Journal of Personality and Social Psychology, 5, 24-31.

Myers, D. G. (1978). The human puzzle: Psychological research and Christian belief. San Francisco: Harper & Row.

Orne, M. T. (1962). On the social psychology of the psychological experiment: With particular reference to demand characteristics and their implications. American Psychologist, 17, 776-783.

Patton, M. (1984). Managing social interactions in counseling: A contribution from the philosophy of science. Journal of Counseling Psychology, 31, 442-456.

Pepinsky, H. B., & Pepinsky, P. (1954). Counseling: Theory and practice. New York: Ronald.

Rogers, C. R. (1961). On becoming a person: A therapist's view of psychotherapy. Boston: Houghton Mifflin.

Rorty, R. (1979). Philosophy and the mirror of nature. Princeton N.J.: Princeton University Press.

Rychlak, J. F. (1979). Discovering free will and personal responsibility. New York: Oxford University Press.

Sarbin, T. R. (Ed.) (1986). Narrative psychology: The storied nature of human conduct. New York: Praeger.

Schachter, S. (1982). Recidivism and self-cure of smoking and obesity. American Psychologist, 37, 436-444.

Schelling, T. C. (1978). Micromotives and macrobehavior. New York: Norton.

Schumacher, E. F. (1973). Small is beautiful. New York: Harper & Row.

Schwartz, B. (1986). The battle for human nature. New York: Norton.

Secord, P. F. (1984). Determinism, free will and self-intervention: A psychological perspective. New Ideas in Psychology, 2, 250-33.

Skinner, B. F. (1971). Beyond freedom and dignity. New York: Alfred Knopf.

Smith, B. D., & Vetter, H. J. (1982). Theoretical approaches to personality. Englewood Cliffs, N.J.: Prentice-Hall.

Steibe, S. C., & Howard, G. S. (1986). The volitional treatment of bulimia. The Counseling Psychologist, 14, 85-94.

Steiner, C. M. (1974). Scripts people live. New York: Bantam Books.

Strupp, H. H. (1977). A tripartite model of mental health and therapeutic outcomes: With special reference to negative effects in psychotherapy. American Psychologist, 32, 187-196.

Taylor, R. (1966). Action and purpose. Englewood Cliffs, N.J.:

Prentice-Hall.

Tversky, A., & Kahneman, D. (1974). Judgment under uncertainty: Heuristics and biases.

Valsiner, J. (Ed.) (1986). The individual subject and scientific psychology. New York: Plenum.

van Inwagen, P. (1983). An essay on free will. Oxford: Clarendon.

Van Leeuven, M. S. (1982). The sorcerers' apprentice: A Christian looks at the changing face of psychology. Downers Grove, IL.: Intervarsity Press.

Van Leeuven, M. S. (1988). Psychology's two cultures: A Christian analysis. Paper presented at the University of Notre Dame, April, 1988.

Watson, J. B. (1925). Psychology, from the standpoint of a behaviorist. Philadelphia: Lippencott.

Weber, S. J., & Cook, T. D. (1972). Subject effects in laboratory research: An examination of subject roles, demand characteristics, and valid inference. Psychological Bulletin, 77, 273-295.

Wicklund, R. A. & Brehm, J. W. (1976). Perspectives on cognitive dissonance. Hillsdale, N.J.: Erlbaum.

Wortman, C. B. & Brehm, J. W. (1975). Responses to uncontrollable outcomes: An integration of reactance theory and the learned helplessness model. In L. Berkowitz (Ed.) Advances in experimental social psychology (Vol. 8) (pp. 277-336). New York: Academic Press.

Index

Ace, G., 170
Adler, M., 107
Alf, 13
Allport, G., 46, 138
Aristotle, 8, 12, 31
Bacon, F., 22, 23
Bandura, A., 92, 110, 111
Bannister, D., 60
Barlow, D., 113
Bateson, G., VI, 50
Beck, A., 105
Beethoven, L., 81
Bellah, R. 77
Bellow, S., VI
Berger, P., 109-110
Bierce, A., 119, 120, 122, 124-129
Bird, L., 27
Bocky, Uncle, 16-18, 20, 35, 119
Bone Bags, 58
Brehm, J., 110
Brentano, F., 46
Buber, M., 171
Burrell, D., 138, 143
Campbell, D., 116
Carter, J., 102
Cattell, R., 48
Cohen, J., 112, 143, 170
Conway, C., 48, 93, 97, 106, 167
Cook, T., 82, 97, 98
Cooper, K., 93
Copernicus, 23-24
Curtin, T., 48, 145, 167
Darcy, Father, 39
de Charms, R., 109, 110
Deci, E., 109, 110
Descartes, R., 23
Dewar, J., 122
de Rojas, F., 79
DiGangi, M., 92, 95, 97, 100, 101
Disney, W., 120
Dooley, T., 81

Dragon, The, 15
Dunfee, J., 103
Dunne, J., 143, 171
Earl of Chesterfield, 23
Edwards, O., 171
Einstein, A., 57, 59, 80, 91
Ellis, A., 133, 140
Emerson, R., 166
Evans, C., 171
Farragut, D., 124
Ferre, F., 109
Fields, W., 1
Fishbein, S., 93
Ford, D., 110
Frank, J., 102
Freud, S., 15, 85, 86, 115, 132-139, 166
Friday, Sergeant Joe, 119
Friedman, M., 134
Frost, R., 78
Gabbard, C., 103
Galileo, 23-24, 115
Gelso, C., 102, 112, 113, 170
Gergen, K., 56, 141
Gergen, M., 56
Ghandi, M., 81, 146
Goethe, 7
Goldman, L., 112, 170
Grandma, 35-36
Grusec, J., 110
Gulanick, J., 55, 91, 164
Gulanick, N., 18-20, 121-128, 164
Hall, G., 50
Hammerskjold, D., 81
Harré, R., 109, 111, 112, 138
Harren, V., 20, 53-55, 167
Harts, The, 14, 120
Hayes, S., 113
Heideigger, M., 84
Hericlitus, 141
Horney, K., 132
Howard, George, 25, 48, 54, 93, 97, 102, 103, 106, 108, 112,
    124, 145, 167, 169, 170
Howard, Gregory, 91, 98, 164

Howard, J., 3, 91, 123
Howard, Margaret, 18, 22, 34-42
Howard, Marion, 1, 40
Howard, W., 1, 35
Immergluck, L., 111
James, W., 15, 44, 46, 48, 71, 72, 127, 166
Johnson, A., 48, 92, 95, 97, 100, 145, 167
Johnson, M., 125
Jones, Officer, 3-4
Jordan, Margaret, 34-35, 82
Jordan, Michael, 27
Jung, C., 46, 132
Kahneman, D., 110
Kasschau, R., 18-19
Kelly, G., 46, 138
Kepler, J., 22-23
Kermit the Frog, 165
Keynes, J., 134
Kimble, G., 111
King, M., 81
Knoblach, H., 41
Koch, S., 45, 141
Koufax, S., 1
Kuhn, T., 25
Laffer, A., 134
Lakoff, G., 125
Lamiel, J., 165
Larson, J., 112
Laughery, K., 18-19
Lazarick, D., 93, 107
Lazarus, A., 84, 107
Leary, D., 45, 48
Lefcourt, H., 111
Lewinsohn, P., 106
Loevinger, 85, 86
Loiello, M., 93
Luke, St., 121
MacArthur, D., 14
Mahon, B., 3-4, 20
Mahoney, M., 133
Mair, M., 48, 75
Marcia, 13-14
Marx, K., 115, 133

Maslow, A., 46, 138, 166
Maxwell, S., 82-83
McBroom, A., 172
McDerbys, The, 39
McHale, K., 27
McIntyre, A., 77, 171
McMullin, E., 9-12, 23-24, 70, 80-81, 115, 141, 144
Meara, N., 47
Milgram, S., 97
Miller, W. M., 75
Miller, W. R., 171
Mischel, W., 110
Mother Theresa, 81
Murray, H., 46
Murray, J., 170
Myers, D., 171
Myers, P., 102
Nance, D., 102
Nelson, R., 113
Newton, I., 23-24, 29
Nichols, D., 112
Nietzsche, F., 1, 128, 168
Orne, M., 97
Palmer, A., 17, 119
Patton, M., 102
Pepinsky, H., 113
Pepinsky, P., 113
Phelps, R., 83
Plato, 8, 121
Polkinghorne, D., 48, 50, 73
Pope, A., 24
Pope Urban, 115
Popper, K., 29
Ptolemy, 23
Rafferty, G., VI
Rank, O., 132
Rhyne, J., 166
Rockefeller, J., 121
Rogers, C., 46, 86, 138
Rychlak, J., 46, 130, 142
Sandler, D., 160-161, 164
Sandler, H., 77, 85, 149-164
Sandler, R., 162-164

Sarbin, T., VII, 49, 75
Scarr, S., 82
Schachter, S., 99, 100
Schwartz, B., 77
Schelling, T., 89
Schumacher, E., 89
Secord, P., 54, 109, 138
Selden, J., 123
Shakespeare, W., 3, 55, 76, 81, 117, 131, 147
Shaw, G. B., 171
Siatczynski, A., 93, 97
Skinner, B. F., 111, 115, 116, 132, 143, 166
Smith, B., 167
Steibe, S., 93
Steiner, C., 85
Strupp, H., 116
Tageson, W., 138
Tarico, V., 82
Taversky, A., 110
Taylor, C., 109, 138
Tennyson, A., 124
Thoreson, C., 133
Tony, 13-14, 120
Toulmin, S., 138
Twain, M., 51, 58
Valsiner, J., 165
Van Leeuven, M., 171
Vetter, H., 167
Wager, W., 43
Watson, J., 44, 47
Weber, S., 97
Wicklund, R., 110
Wilde, O, 130
Woolf, V., 166
Wortman, C., 110
Wright, L., 138
Wright, P., 168
Wundt, W., 43-44
Youngs, W., 93, 97
Zhivago, Dr., 121

About the Author

George S. Howard is professor and chairperson of the Department of Psychology at the University of Notre Dame, Notre Dame, Indiana. He received a Ph.D. in counseling psychology in 1975 from Southern Illinois University in Carbondale, Illinois. His research has focused upon theoretical, methodological, and philosophical problems in applied areas of psychological research such as counseling, clinical, educational, and industrial/organizational psychology. A Fellow of Divisions 2, 17, and 24 of the American Psychological Association, he is author of four other books and over a hundred articles in professional journals. He and his wife, Nancy A. Gulanick, are the parents of two sons, John Jordan Gulanick and Gregory Edward Howard.